3:07
July 2018

For Jason,

Whose wisdom —
since his young years—has long blessed
my life, and
with whom I look
forward to working
with,

Dr. Tell...

UNCOMMON SENSE

SENSE

The World's Fullest Compendium of Wisdom

JOSEPH TELUSHKIN

Shapolsky Publishers
56 East 11th Street
New York, NY 10003

A Shapolsky Book

Copyright © 1987 by Joseph Telushkin

For any additional information, contact:
Shapolsky Publishers, Inc.
56 East 11th Street, NY, NY 10003

First Edition 1987

2 3 4 5 6 7 8 9 10

Library of Congress Cataloging in Publication Data

Telushkin, Joseph, 1948-
UNCOMMON SENSE
1. Quotations.   I. Title.
PN6095.J4T4   1986   081   86-60181

ISBN 0-933503-48-2

Book Design by Malcolm Jordan-Robinson
Typography by Shapolsky Compositors

FOR DENNIS PRAGER AND JANICE PRAGER

CONTENTS

6

Acknowledgments

I have discussed the ideas in this book with many people, and to all of them I feel deeply indebted. There are a few names, however, that I wish to mention with special gratitude.

Dennis Prager and I have been friends for over twenty years. Our friendship has been in equal measures both emotional and intellectual. The emotional element accounts for my dedicating this book to him and his wife, Janice. The intellectual element prompts me to acknowledge that the philosophy of life and religion that I hold, and which determined the contents of this book, was in large measure worked out in 3 A.M. discussions with him.

I would like to thank my editor, Linda Kachani, for her meticulous and skillful work. Her emendations, original suggestions and editorial improvements have touched every page of this book. She has saved me from errors of judgment as well as of style, and has made the text more readable and logical. Every writer should be blessed with such an editor.

I am also very happy to be able to express publicly my thanks to Ian Shapolsky, Eve Gittelson and Jeff Schaire of Shapolsky Publishers for their commitment to, and hard work with me on *Uncommon Sense*. Their faith in the book has deeply moved me, while their suggestions have greatly improved the manuscript.

Author's Preface

Much of what most people call "common sense" may well be *nonsense*. In any case, I think it's high time we took a hard look at some common "truisms" to see if they have held up over time.

Several years ago, for example, a large Protestant organization took out a two-page advertisement in *Newsweek*. Three words dominated the page: LOVE YOUR ENEMY. Evidently, this is what the organization believed *Newsweek's* millions of readers most needed to hear. Jesus's injunction in Matthew has, in fact, for two thousand years largely determined Christianity's response to evil people. In 1981, when the world was shocked by Ali Agca's attempted assassination of Pope John Paul II, the Pope announced – just four days after the shooting – that he forgave his attacker, even though Agca himself (who, coincidentally, had previously murdered another person) had not asked for forgiveness.

I believe that it is worth taking a look at the rationale of those who *oppose* loving one's enemies, as well as another look at the words of those who have subjected other clichés of received wisdom to the kind of scrutiny that has been educated by history. That's why I have called this book *Uncommon Sense*.

* * * * *

Uncommon Sense ranges over 3,000 years of the best thoughts of the brightest people to challenge the idea that one should love one's enemies, as well as other widely held beliefs. The spectrum of subjects covered is as broad as life itself, but my selections have been governed by some general theories, all of which to some extent defy popular wisdom.

I do not believe that human beings are born good; I believe that they must be educated to goodness. The dominant Western view (stemming from Jean Jacques Rousseau's and the Enlightenment's concept of the "natural man") that people are born "good" and then corrupted by "society," is, I think, false. This idea has led us to blame institutions, and try to change them, rather than human beings. I believe that it is human beings who corrupt social institutions, not the reverse. At the heart of this view of the world is the biblical verse, "The tendency of man's heart is towards evil from his youth" (Genesis 8:21). People are *not* naturally good, the Bible tells us, and evil behavior is not solely the province of the mentally disturbed.

This issue has massive social ramifications. For example, those who believe that people are basically good generally also favor value-free education. After all, if people naturally gravitate to the good, they do not need to learn values. Just give them the facts, and of course they'll do what's right.

But one who accepts the Biblical view of human nature realizes that education alone will not induce good behavior. Consider the prominent academics and intellectuals who supported and worked for the Nazi Party, or the fact that more than half of the leaders of the Einsatzgruppen – the mobile killing units of the Nazis that murdered over a million Jews in Russia – held advanced degrees. This is merely a single example. The list goes on and on. That is why human values must be *taught*. For just as we won't have good chemists or pianists if we don't teach piano or chemistry, so, too, we won't have good people if we don't teach goodness.

• • • • •

Similarly, although democratic societies tend to operate as if it weren't so, I believe, as Alexander Solzhenitsyn said in his 1978 Harvard Commencement speech, that "it is time in the West to defend not so much human rights as human obligations."

A society will only be able to survive as long as its citizens are as conscious of their obligations as they are of their rights. In contemporary America, stress is placed almost exclusively on the rights of the individual; the country was founded, of course, on the basis of protecting inalienable rights. But, for example, it has been the right to free speech exercised irresponsibly and without a sense of moral obligation, which has on occasion led to massive suffering, murder, even genocide.

I believe that without acknowledging our obligations, democratic society is doomed. Edith Hamilton's description of the fall of Athens may someday be applied to us. "When the freedom they wished for most was the freedom from responsibility, then Athens ceased to be free and never was free again."

Obviously, this belief applies only to democratic societies. In those countries whose leaders speak *solely* of obligations, while denying their citizens the most basic human rights, all efforts must be focused on first gaining those rights. But as far as the free Western world is concerned, as an Argentinian carpenter named Antonio Porchis said, "God has given a great deal to man, but man would like something from man."

• • • • •

I believe that all morality is based on God. Most secular Westerners, in spite of massive evidence to the contrary, are convinced that education and reason have replaced God as the agencies through which people become good. Education and reason, however, are fundamentally limited in their ability to instill moral values. Although they can answer many questions, the world has paid a huge price in human suffering to learn that there is one question neither reason nor education can ever answer: Why be good?

Only a belief in God allows us to answer that question with any certainty. As Dostoevsky said, "If there is no God, all is permitted.

• • • • •

I believe, also, that man's task is to perfect the world, but that in most cases this must be achieved slowly, by evolution rather than revolution. In Western countries, right-wing ideologues generally romanticize the past, and left-wing ideologues romanticize the future. Both ideologies are united in their implicit repudiation of the present.

The right wing speaks of the "good old days." But whoever thought they were good at the time? As critic Brooks Atkinson said, "Every age has consisted of crises that seemed intolerable to the people who lived through them."

Conversely, the left wing wishes to dissolve the present in favor of some Utopian future. But, ironically, the Utopias the left has established have been Utopian for one class only – the ruling class. Soviet Communism is the classic example: in the name of this faith over twenty million people have been murdered. In East Germany, the government puts up barbed wire fences, and posts guards with machine guns to prevent citizens from leaving.

Rabbi Wolf of Strikov said, "You are not as good as you think you are, and the world is not as bad as you think it is." This should be heeded by Utopians of both the right and the left.

The voices that resonate through *Uncommon Sense* are those of people committed to making the world a better place. But their methods are evolutionary. They know where revolutionary transformations lead – to the French Reign of Terror, to the Soviet GULAG, to the horrors of Auschwitz and Dachau, to the mass murders in Kampuchea.

Listen to Albert Camus: "Perhaps we cannot prevent this world from being a world in which children are tortured. But we can reduce the number of tortured children." Listen to the second-century Rabbi Tarfon, "It is not your obligation to complete the work [of perfecting the world], but neither are you free from doing all you can."

· · · · ·

In addition to being a credo, *Uncommon Sense* is also a commonplace book. Included within it are many quotations that, while deeply insightful, are leavened with the humor of the human comedy. Some are just plain funny, some fly in the face of traditional notions of wisdom – but when you look a bit closer I believe you'll be able to discern the seeds of profound truth. As Freud said, jokes come from the deepest levels of our unconscious.

I've divided *Uncommon Sense* into sections that are based on the traditional categories of the Jewish commandments, "between man and man," and "between man and God." I've also found it useful to add two categories of my own: "between man and himself," and "between man and the world." These are, of course, merely permutations of the original categories.

BETWEEN MAN AND MAN

LOVE YOUR ENEMIES?

Love your enemies and pray for those who persecute you . . .
for if you love those who love you, what right have you to claim
any credit?

Jesus
(Matthew 5:44, 48)

Because these words have so influenced Christianity and western
notions of right and wrong, it is worth taking a look at the
rationales of those who oppose loving one's enemies and
persecutors.

Someone asked Confucius, "What do you think of repaying evil
with kindness?" Confucius replied, "Then what are you going to
repay kindness with? Repay kindness with kindness but repay evil
with justice."

Confucius
(Analects)

Can there be love which does not make demands upon its object?
Confucius
(Analects)

He who is merciful when he should be cruel will in the end be
cruel when he should be merciful.

Midrash Samuel
(Jewish rabbinic text
from early Middle Ages)

The discussion about cruelty and mercy, from which the above quote derives, occurs in a commentary on the book of Samuel I. In Chapter 15, King Saul is commanded by God to kill his prisoner Agag, the murderous king of Amalek. Saul does not do so, out of a combination of mercy and respect for a fellow monarch. As punishment, God instructs the Prophet Samuel to replace Saul with David. When Saul realizes he will lose his kingdom, he becomes furious. The king, who was too merciful to kill the murderer Agag, then goes on to murder eighty-five innocent priests of the city of Nob for giving David a night's lodging (Chapter 22).

This biblical story is one of many historical instances in which misplaced mercy has led to subsequent cruelty. In March, 1917, Alexander Kerensky helped to overthrow the Czar and establish the first democratic government in Russian history. Kerensky even allowed Lenin and the anti-democratic Bolsheviks to operate freely. Lenin repaid Kerensky's kindness by overthrowing his government in November. Kerensky fled to New York where he lived out his life in exile. It is the Russian people who live under Communist rule who have paid the price for Kerensky's mercifulness.

Instead of loving your enemies, treat your friends a little better.
Edgar Watson Howe
(American journalist and author,
in his book *Plain People*)

You needn't love your enemy, but if you refrain from telling lies about him, you are doing well enough.
Edgar Watson Howe

To an ordinary human being love means nothing if it does not mean loving some people more than others.

George Orwell

Tell me whom you love and I will tell you what you are.

Arsène Houssaye

A man is only as good as what he loves.

Saul Bellow
(Seize the Day)

Bellow's words should be kept in mind when we hear of "good" people who are the friends of vicious people, or who support immoral political movements. A reader of the biographies of Adolf Hilter, for instance, might form the impression that the woman who loved him and lived with him, Eva Braun, was an essentially sweet, if politically naïve, woman. The single most revealing thing we know about Eva Braun, however, is that she loved Adolf Hitler.

LOVE YOUR NEIGHBOR

Love thy neighbor as thyself, but choose your neighborhood.
Louis Beal

Eric Hoffer, longshoreman and political scientist, has said that the Bible commanded the love of neighbor rather than of mankind because it is easier to love humanity as a whole than to love one's neighbor.

In China, an American woman journalist watched a frail Sister cleansing the gangrenous sores of wounded soldiers.

"I wouldn't do that for a million dollars," the visitor remarked.

Without a pause in her work the Sister replied, "Neither would I."
Catholic Digest

Tse Kung asked Confucius, "What would you say if all the people in a village like a person?"

"That is not enough," replied Confucius.

"What would you say if all the people in a village dislike a person?"

"That is not enough," said Confucius. "It is better when the good people of a village like him, and the bad people of the village dislike him. When you are disliked by the bad persons, you are a good person.

Lin Yutang
(The Wisdom of Confucius)

Rabbi Moshe Leib of Sassov said: How to love men is something I learned from a peasant. He was sitting in an inn along with other peasants, drinking. For a long time he was silent as all the rest, but when he was moved by the wine, he asked one of the men seated beside him: "Tell me, do you love me or don't you love me?" The other replied: "I love you very much." But the first peasant replied: "You say that you love me, but you do not know what I need. If you really loved me you would know." The other had not a word to say to this, and the peasant who had put the question fell silent again. But I understood. To know the needs of men and to bear the burden of their sorrow – that is the true love of men.

Martin Buber
(Tales of the Hasidim – Later Masters)

ROMANTIC LOVE

I did not know I loved you till I heard myself telling you so –
for one instant I thought, "Good God, what have I said?" – and
then I knew it was the truth.

Bertrand Russell
(in a letter to Ottoline Morrell)

If we discovered that we had only five minutes left to say all we
wanted to say, every telephone booth would be occupied by
people calling each other to stammer that they loved them.

Christopher Morley

We love those we are happy with. We do. For how else can we
know we love them, or how else define loving?

Nan Fairbrother

The greatest happiness of life is the conviction that we are
loved – loved for ourselves, or rather, loved in spite of ourselves.

Victor Hugo

A loveless world is a dead world, and always there comes an hour
when one is weary of. . . one's work, and of devotion to duty, and
all one cares for is a loved face, the warmth and wonder of a
loving heart.

Albert Camus
(The Plague)

Le coeur a ses raisons que la raison ne connait pas.
The heart has its reasons that reason does not know.

Blaise Pascal
(Pensées)

Only God, my dear,
Could love you for yourself alone
And not your yellow hair

William Butler Yeats
("For Anne Gregory")

Meanwhile, love, except as comic relief, between a short fat man and a flat-chested girl is still beyond the limits of the movies.

Mordecai Richler

The magic of first love is our ignorance that it can ever end.

Benjamin Disraeli
(Henrietta Temple)

When I was sixteen more than anything else in the world I wanted to be a success when I grew up. I did not know there was any other way of being lovable.

Harold Brodkey
(First Love and Other Sorrows)

Love: Its Down Side

When a man of forty falls in love with a girl of twenty, it isn't her youth he is seeking but his own.

Lenore Coffee
(quoted in John Robert Colombo's
book *Popcorn in Paradise*)

It is seldom indeed that one parts on good terms, because if one were on good terms one would not part.

Marcel Proust
(The Fugitive)

Lovers who have nothing to do but love each other are not really to be envied; love and nothing else very soon is nothing else.

Walter Lippman
(A Preface to Morals)

And to think that I have wasted several years of my life, and that I have wanted to die, that I have had my greatest love, for a woman who was not my kind.

Marcel Proust
(quoted in Dorothy Tennov's
book *Love and Limerance*)

I don't want people to love me. It makes for obligations.

Jean Anouilh
(The Lark)

Unrequited Love: Both Sides

Then you reach the final torment: utter despair poisoned still further by a shred of hope.

Stendahl
[pseudonym of Marie Henri Beyle]
(Love)

Madame: I was told that you took the trouble to come here to see me three times last evening. I was not in. And, fearing lest persistence expose you to humiliation, I am bound by rules of politeness to warn you that *I shall never be in.*

Gustave Flaubert
(to a former lover)

And if I loved you Wednesday
Well, what is that to you?
I do not love you Thursday
So much is true.

Edna St. Vincent Millay
(Thursday)

When a man has once loved a woman he will do anything for her except continue to love her.

Oscar Wilde
(An Ideal Husband)

MARRIAGE AND ITS DISCONTENTS

We sleep in separate rooms, we have dinner apart, we take separate vacations – we're doing everything we can to keep our marriage together.

Rodney Dangerfield

When I was a young man I vowed never to marry until I found the ideal woman. Well, I found her – but alas, she was waiting for the ideal man.

Robert Schuman
(a former French Foreign Minister)

As a general thing, people marry most happily with their own kind. The trouble lies in the fact that people usually marry at an age when they do not really know what their own kind is.

Robertson Davies
(A Voice From the Attic)

Before you marry make sure you know whom you are going to divorce.

Yiddish proverb
(quoted in Hanan Ayalti's
Yiddish Proverbs)

When a divorced man marries a divorced woman, there are four minds in bed.

Talmud
(Tractate *Pesahim* 112a)

In the course of his sermon, [the preacher] asserted that the Savior was the only perfect man who had ever appeared in this world, also that there was no record in the Bible, or elsewhere, of any perfect woman having lived on this earth. Whereupon there arose in the rear of the Church a persecuted-looking personage who said, "I know a perfect woman, and for the last six years." "Who was she?" asked the minister. "My husband's first wife," replied the afflicted female.

Abraham Lincoln
(quoted in Carl Sandburg's
Abraham Lincoln: The War Years)

Many a man owes his success to his first wife and his second wife to his success.

Jim Backus

One problem is that we have no reference points. All our traditions are crumbling. Look at the Catholic Church. The only people who want to get married today are Catholic priests.

Mortimer Feinberg
(quoted in *Business Week,*
March 10, 1975)

No man is a hero to his wife's psychiatrist.

Dr. Eric Berne
(psychiatrist and author of
Games People Play)

Berne was, of course, updating the proverb, "No man is a hero to his valet," concerning which **Friedrich Hegel** wrote, "This is not because the hero is no hero but because the valet is a valet."

BETWEEN MEN AND WOMEN:
THE GOOD, THE BAD AND THE UGLY

If women didn't exist, all the money in the world would have no meaning.

Aristotle Onassis

He who believes in nothing still needs a woman to believe in him.

Eugene Rosenstock-Huesey

A woman without a man is like a fish without a bicycle.

American feminist slogan

Whatever women do they must do twice as well as men to be thought half as good. Luckily, this is not difficult.

Charlotte Whitton
(on her election as
the mayor of Ottawa)

When a woman behaves like a man, why can't she behave like a nice man?

Dame Edith Evans

Humans are not a very loving species – especially when they make love. Too bad.

Dr. Robert Stoller
(Sexual Imagination)

The man's most masculine part is also the most easily intimidated.

Robert Musil
(quoted in George Gilder's
book *Sexual Suicide*)

A man doesn't rape for sex any more than an alcoholic drinks because he's thirsty.

Dr. A. Nicholas Groth
(Director of the Sex Offenders Program for
Connecticut's Department of Corrections,
New York Times, February 5, 1980)
Groth concludes, therefore, that "rape is
not the aggressive expression of sexuality
[but] the sexual expression of aggression."

In the early years of the state of Israel a number of rapes occurred, and at a cabinet meeting one member proposed that women not be allowed out alone at night until the rapists were caught. **Golda Meir,** the only female member of the cabinet, was asked her opinion. "I don't understand the proposal," she said. "Men are committing the rapes. Men should not be allowed out at night."

George Bernard Shaw once asked a beautiful woman, "Would you sleep with me for a million pounds?"

"Yes," she answered.

"Would you sleep with me for five pounds?"

"What do you think I am?" she flared.

"We've already established that," said Shaw. "Now we're just haggling over the price."

Ninety percent of all Christians practice polygamy – only they don't call it that.

Mormon from Utah
(quoted in *Newsweek*,
November 21, 1977)

Literature is mostly about sex and not much about having children and life is the other way around.

David Lodge
(The British Museum is Falling Down)

The most important trait in a woman is whatever trait the woman you are going out with is lacking.

Joseph Telushkin

The above, which obviously applies to both sexes, occurred to me when a friend explained for the fifth time in as many months why he was ending yet another relationship. The first woman was not particularly bright and he concluded that there was nothing more important in a woman than brains. This conclusion lasted until the next woman turned out to be cold, and I was told that warmth was what mattered most. The next woman was not attractive enough, her successor was not kind, and the next was an unhappy person. Each in turn prompted a new conclusion as to what was the most important trait in a woman.

I'm a practicing heterosexual. . . but bisexuality immediately doubles your chances for a date on Saturday night.

Woody Allen

FRIENDSHIP

Would you know who is your friend and who is your enemy?
Note what is in your own heart.

Solomon Ibn Gabirol
(medieval Jewish philosopher,
in his *Pearls of Wisdom*)

If you want to discover your true opinion of anybody, observe the
impression made on you by the first sight of a letter from him.

Arthur Schopenhauer
The contemporary equivalent
would be assessing your reaction
when you hear his voice on
your answering machine.

If I am pressed to say why I loved him, I feel it can only be
explained by replying "Because it was he; because it was me."

Michel de Montaigne

We never know the true value of friends. While they live we are
too sensitive of their faults; when we have lost them we only see
their virtues.

J. C. and A. W. Hare
(Guesses At Truth, 1827)

My friend is he who will tell me my faults in private.

Solomon Ibn Gabirol
(Pearls of Wisdom)

BETWEEN PARENTS AND CHILDREN

Parents give you advice and never stop to think of what you think of what they turned out to be.

Harold Brodkey
(First Love and Other Sorrows)

Nothing has a stronger influence psychologically on their environment, and especially on their children, than the unlived life of the parents.

Carl Jung

What a father says to his children is not heard by the world, but it will be heard by posterity.

Jean Paul Richter
(German humorist)

Depression is being noticed by my mother in public and ignored by her in private.

**Suicide note of Dolores, a
twenty-three-year-old girl**
(quoted in Edwin Schneidman's
Voices of Death)

Parentage is a very important profession; but no test of fitness for it is ever imposed in the interest of the children.

George Bernard Shaw
(Everybody's Political What's What)

> A friend's father used to point out
> that in New York you have to have
> a license to sell bagels, while
> anybody with a sexual organ is
> permitted to have children.

There are no illegitimate children – only illegitimate parents.
> **Judge Leon Yankwich**
> (1928)

Unfortunately, as **Bergen Evans** writes: "Judge Yankwich's dictum does honor to his heart," but bears no relationship to how illegitimacy has been judged throughout history (*Dictionary of Quotations*).

The most important thing a father can do for his children is to love their mother.
> **Reverend Theodore Hesburgh**
> (President of Notre Dame)

Children have never been very good at listening to their elders, but they have never failed to imitate them.
> **James Baldwin**

He who does not teach his son a profession teaches him to be a thief.
> **Talmud**
> (Tractate *Kiddushin* 30b)

When a father gives to his son, both laugh. When a son gives to his father, both cry.

Yiddish proverb

A Jewish man with parents alive is a fifteen-year-old boy, and will remain a fifteen-year-old boy until they die.

Philip Roth
(Portnoy's Complaint)

A characteristic Jewish joke tells of three elderly Jewish women sitting on a bench in Miami Beach, each bragging about how devoted her son is. The first woman says: "Last year, for my seventieth birthday, my son gave me an all-expense paid cruise around the world. First class." The second woman says: "My son is more devoted. For my birthday last year he catered an affair in my honor. He even flew my close friends in from New York." The third woman says: "My son is the most devoted. Three times a week he goes to a psychiatrist. One hundred and ten dollars an hour he pays him. And what does he speak about the whole time? Me!"

We should not make light of the troubles of children. They are worse than ours, because we can see the end of our trouble and they can never see any end.

William Middleton
(quoted in William Butler Yeats's
Autobiography)

When I was a boy of fourteen my father was so ignorant I could hardly stand to have the old man around. But when I got to be twenty-one I was astonished at how much the old man had learned in seven years.

Mark Twain

Children begin by loving their parents. After a time they judge them. Rarely, if ever, do they forgive them.

Oscar Wilde
(A Woman of No Importance)

The often confused mixture of emotions that children feel for parents perhaps accounts for the peculiar fact that the **Bible** legislates love of neighbor (Leviticus 19:18), of stranger (Leviticus 19:34), and of God (Deuteronomy 6:5), but not of parents. In so intimate a relationship love is too volatile an emotion to be commanded; therefore, the Bible demands a standard of honor and respect ("Honor your father and mother" – Exodus 20:12) that can remain in force even in times of estrangement.

All happy families are alike, but each unhappy family is unhappy in its own way.

Leo Tolstoy
(Anna Karenina)

No matter how many communes anybody invents, the family always creeps back.

Margaret Mead

No man ever said on his deathbed, "I wish I had spent more time on my business."

Sen. Paul Tsongas
The Senator used this quote
from a friend, to explain
his decision to leave the
Senate and spend more
time with his family, after
learning that he had cancer.

Why do grandparents and grandchildren get along so well together? Perhaps the best answer is the one I heard from a psychiatrist recently: "Because they have a common enemy – the parents."

Sydney Harris
(Leaving the Surface)

TRUTH AND LIES

Lies

The liar's punishment is not in the least that he is not believed, but that he cannot believe anyone else.

George Bernard Shaw

If you have reason to suspect that a person is telling you a lie, look as though you believed every word he said. This will give him the courage to go on; he will become more vehement in his assertions, and in the end betray himself.

Arthur Schopenhauer
(Our Relation to Others)

Liars share with those they deceive the desire not to be deceived.

Sissela Bok
(Lying)

If you tell the truth you don't have to remember anything.

Mark Twain

Rabbi Naftali of Rotchitz remarked of a man who was a well-known liar: "Not only is what he says untrue, but even the opposite of what he says is untrue."

Shmuel Avidor Ha-Cohen
(Touching Heaven Touching Earth)

Novelist **Mary McCarthy** recently directed a contemporary version of this comment at playwright Lillian Hellman. On "The Dick Cavett Show," McCarthy declared: "Every word Lillian Hellman writes is a lie and that includes the words 'and' and 'the'." Hellman responded with a lawsuit.

Nobody has a right to put another under such a difficulty that he must either hurt the person by telling the truth, or hurt himself by telling what is not true.

Samuel Johnson

If I accustom a servant to tell a lie for me, have I not reason to apprehend that he will tell many lies for *himself*?

Samuel Johnson
Substitute child for servant
and note the contemporary
relevance of this statement.

It is hard to believe that a man is telling the truth when you know that you would lie if you were in his place.

H. L. Mencken

The great masses of the people will fall more easily victim to a big lie than a small one.

Adolf Hitler

Remember, one lie does not cost you one truth, but the truth.

Friedrich Hebbel

A Time To Lie?

The General Rule is that truth should never be violated; there must however be some exceptions. If, for instance, a murderer should ask you which way a man has gone.

Samuel Johnson

Optimistic lies have such immense therapeutic value that a doctor who cannot tell them convincingly has mistaken his profession.

George Bernard Shaw
(Misalliance)

Johnson and Shaw stand in a long tradition that asserts there are justifiable lies, certainly when human life is at stake. In the **Bible,** God not only condones but actually sanctions such lies. When He commands the Prophet Samuel to annoint David as king in place of Saul, Samuel demurs: "How can I go? If Saul hears about it, he will kill me." God does not promise Samuel protection, nor does He tell him to speak truthfully and bear the consequences. He instructs him to tell Saul a lie, that he is going away to offer a sacrifice (I Samuel 16:2). Apparently, God wished to teach Samuel that one does not owe would-be murderers the truth.

This seemingly unexceptional bit of biblical wisdom has been challenged by at least two philosophical giants: **St. Augustine** and **Immanuel Kant.** Augustine believed that telling a lie costs a person eternal life, and that lying to save a human life is therefore foolish and unjustifiable. "Does he not speak most perversely who says that one person ought to die spiritually so another may live? . . . . Since then, eternal life is lost by lying, a lie may never be told for the preservation of the temporal life of another" ("On Lying," in *Treatises on Various Subjects*). In response to Augustine's prohibition, Catholic tradition introduced the concept of the "mental reservation." So, when a feverish patient asks a doctor what his temperature is, for instance, the doctor may respond, "Your temperature is normal today," while making the "mental reservation" that it is normal for someone in the patient's precise physical condition (Charles McFadden, *Medical Ethics*).

For Kant, truth was a universal moral absolute, allowing for no exceptions. He contended that if a would-be murderer inquires whether "our friend who is pursued by him had taken refuge in our house" we are forbidden to lie ("On a Supposed Right to Lie from Benevolent Motives," in *The Critique of Practical Reason*). Philosopher **Sissela Bok** points out in *Lying* that according to Kant's ethics the captain of a ship transporting fugitives from Nazi Germany would be forbidden to lie to a patroling Nazi vessel that asked him whether he had Jews aboard. Most non-Augustinians and non-Kantians find this moral obligation, to tell murderers a truth that will help them murder, as itself immoral.

Truth

God forbid that truth should be confined to Mathematical Demonstration.

William Blake
(notes on Reynold's *Discourses*, 1808)

Blake was one of the early English Romantics, the movement that rebelled against the Neo-classical focus on rationalism and science. The problem Blake raised is still reflected in contemporary philosophy, in which, on the major issues of life, truth is often seen as relative, while certainty is confined to more trivial and insignificant issues.

Truth is on the march; nothing can stop it now.

Emile Zola
("J'accuse")

Zola's exuberant prophecy was happily fulfilled. "J'accuse," his denunciation of the infamous government and military conspiracy that falsely imprisoned the Jewish French army officer Alfred Dreyfus on Devil's Island, helped exonerate Dreyfus and effect his release. Zola, meanwhile, had to flee France to escape imprisonment for "libeling" the government.

How often I have said to you that when you have eliminated the impossible, whatever remains, however improbable, must be the truth.

Sir Arthur Conan Doyle
(The Sign of Four)

There was truth and there was untruth and if you clung to the truth even against the whole world you were not mad.

George Orwell

He did not publish his book until he was on his deathbed. He knew how dangerous it is to be right when the rest of the world is wrong.

Thomas B. Reed
(speaking of the Polish astronomer
Copernicus in 1855)

Truth never dies but it lives a wretched life.

Yiddish proverb

As scarce as the truth is, the supply is always greater than the demand.

Josh Billings
(Affurisms, 1865)

Plato is dear to me, but dearer still is truth.

Aristotle
(attributed)

Man wants to be great and sees that he is little; wants to be happy and sees that he is miserable; wants to be perfect and sees that he is full of imperfections; wants to be the object of the love and esteem of men and sees that his faults merit only their...

contempt. The embarrassment in which he finds himself produces the most unjust and criminal passions imaginable, for he conceives a mortal hatred against the truth, which blames him and convinces him of his faults.

Blaise Pascal
(Pensées)

Am I therefore to become your enemy, because I tell you the truth?
The New Testament
(Galatians 4:16)

Truth is too naked; she does not inflame men.

Jean Cocteau
(Cock and Harlequin)
It is almost impossible to forge
a large movement based on reason.
Masses of people can apparently
get passionate only over irrational
or anti-rational movements.

The opposite of a correct statement is a false statement. But the opposite of a profound truth may well be another profound truth.
Niels Bohr
(Nobel Prize-winning physicist)

One thinks different things about the same things in the morning and in the evening. But where is truth, in the night thought or in the spirit of midday?

Albert Camus
(Notebooks, 1935-1942)

A half-truth is a whole lie.

Yiddish proverb

Truth is stranger than fiction because fiction has to make sense.

Mark Twain

HONEST TO GOODNESS

Honesty is the best policy; but he who is governed by that maxim is not an honest man.

Richard Whately
(English logician and theologian;
1787-1863)

I'm afraid we must make the world honest before we can honestly say to our children that honesty is the best policy.

George Bernard Shaw

It is a fine thing to be honest, but it is also very important to be right.

Winston Churchill

On the whole, human beings want to be good, but not too good and not quite all the time.

George Orwell

We think for a landlady considering a lodger it is important to know his income, but still more important to know his philosophy.

G. K. Chesterton
(English Catholic writer and critic)

Chesterton understood that an
honest person, though temporarily
without funds, will eventually
pay his debts, while a dishonest
person, though affluent, will
find ways to cheat his debtor.

Goodness

How wonderful it is that nobody need wait a single moment
before starting to improve the world.

Anne Frank

She also wrote, "Human worth does not lie in riches or power, but
in character or goodness. . . . If people would only begin to
develop this goodness, instead of stifling it, and give the poor
some human sympathy, one would need no money or possessions, for not everyone has that to give away."

In Germany they came first for the Communists, and I didn't
speak up because I wasn't a Communist. Then they came for the
Jews, and I didn't speak up because I wasn't a Jew. Then they
came for the trade unionists, and I didn't speak up because I
wasn't a trade unionist. Then they came for me, and by that time
no one was left to speak up.

Bishop Martin Niemoller

At the Day of Judgment we shall not be asked what we have read
but what we have done.

Thomas à Kempis
(The Imitation of Christ)

Let a good man do good deeds with the same zeal that the evil man does bad ones.

Hasidic saying
(attributed to the Belzer Rebbe)

Keep doing good deeds long enough, and you'll probably turn out a good man. In spite of yourself.

Louis Auchincloss
(The Rector of Justin)

We judge ourselves by our motives and others by their actions.

Dwight Morrow

One cannot weep for the entire world, it is beyond human strength. One must choose.

Jean Anouilh
(Ceceile)

EVIL

It is tempting to deny the existence of evil since denying it obviates
the need to fight it.

Alexis Carrel
(Reflections on Life)
Hence the attempt by many
European politicians to deny
the evil of Nazism in the 1930s,
and similar attempts today to deny
the evils of Soviet Communism.

It seems the world was divided into good and bad people. The
good ones slept better. . . while the bad ones seemed to enjoy the
waking hours much more.

Woody Allen
(Side Effects)

If a man has beheld evil, he may know that it was shown to him in
order that he learn his own guilt and repent; for what is shown to
him is also within him.

Rabbi Israel Baal Shem Tov

All that is necessary for the triumph of evil is for good men to
do nothing.

Edmund Burke
(attributed)

One of the most widely cited of all quotations, no one has yet found this anywhere in Burke's writings. Emily Morison Beck, editor of *Bartlett's Familiar Quotations*, 15th edition, suggests that it is a twentieth-century paraphrase of Burke's view that "When bad men combine, the good must associate; else they will fall one by one" (*Thoughts on the Cause of the Present Discontent*, April 23, 1770).

Jesse James murdered children, but only in fact, not legend.

Unknown

There are a thousand hacking at the branches of evil to one who is striking at the roots.

Henry David Thoreau
(Walden)

Moralist and philosopher **Abraham Joshua Heschel,** writing about the rise of Nazism, expressed the same insight through a parable. A tale is told of a band of inexperienced mountain climbers. Without guides, they struck recklessly into the wilderess. Suddenly a rocky ledge gave way beneath their feet and they tumbled headlong into a dismal pit. In the darkness of the pit they recovered from their shock only to find themselves set upon by a swarm of angry snakes. For each snake the desperate men slew, ten more seemed to lash out in its place. Strangely enough, one man seemed to stand aside from the fight. When indignant voices of his struggling companions reproached him for not fighting, he called back: "If we remain here, we shall be dead before the snakes. I am searching for a way of escape from the pit for all of us." ("The Meaning of this Hour," in *Man's Quest for God*.)

There can be no such thing as a necessary evil. For if a thing is really necessary, it cannot be an evil, and if it is an evil, it is not necessary.

Tiorio

The best lack all conviction, while the worst
Are full of passionate intensity.

William Butler Yeats
(The Second Coming)

When choosing between two evils, I always like to try the one I've never tried before.

Mae West
(in the movie *Klondike Annie*)

HYPOCRISY

Whenever I hear anyone arguing for slavery, I feel a strong impulse to see it tried on him personally.

Abraham Lincoln
(to an Indiana regiment,
March 17, 1865)

Lincoln's criticism could equally well be applied to twentieth-century defenders of totalitarianism. When Lincoln Steffens returned from a visit to the newly established Bolshevik government, he declared: "I am a patriot for Russia, the Future is there; Russia will win out and it will save the world. That is my belief. But I don't want to live there." In 1931, George Bernard Shaw announced as he was leaving the Soviet Union, "Tomorrow I leave this country of hope and return to our Western countries of despair." Shaw never did ask his hosts why their "country of hope" prohibited any Russians from joining him on his masochistic journey from hope to despair.

When the missionaries arrived, the Africans had the land and the missionaries had the Bible. They taught us to pray with our eyes closed. When we opened them, they had the land and we had the Bible.

Jomo Kenyetta
(President of Kenya)

Your health is bound to be affected if, day after day, you say the opposite of what you feel, if you grovel before what you dislike, and rejoice at what brings you nothing but misfortune.

Boris Pasternak
The author of *Dr. Zhivago*,
refused permission by the
Soviet Union to accept the
Nobel Price for Literature
in 1958, is depicting
life under Communism.

He is the kind of politician who would cut down a redwood tree and then mount the stump to make a speech for conservation.

Adlai Stevenson
(attacking Richard Nixon
in a campaign speech, 1956)

When I sell liquor it's called bootlegging; when my patrons serve it on silver trays on Lake Shore Drive, it's called hospitality.

Al Capone

We ought to see far enough into a hypocrite to see even his sincerity.

G. K. Chesterton
(Heretics)

Don't stay away from church because there are so many hypocrites there. There's always room for one more.

A. R. Adams

STICKS AND STONES AND WORDS

The gossiper stands in Syria and kills in Rome.

Jerusalem Talmud,
Peah 1:1

Children chant "Sticks and stones may break my bones, but names can never hurt me." Adults know better – that throughout history, people have always used names and words to incite others to pick up sticks and stones and knives and guns to hurt other people.

Words, of course, can also hurt individuals in another way. A nineteenth-century Jewish folktale tells of a man who went through his community slandering the rabbi. One day, feeling suddenly remorseful, he begged the rabbi for forgiveness and said that he was willing to undergo any penance to make amends. The rabbi told him to take a feather pillow from his home, cut it open, and scatter the feathers to the winds. The man did so immediately, and then went back to the rabbi. The rabbi said, "Now go and gather all the feathers."

"But that's impossible, Rabbi. The wind has already scattered them."

The rabbi answered, "And though you truly wish to correct the evil you have done, it is as impossible to repair the damage done by your words as it is to recover the feathers."

When a man tells you what people are saying about you, tell him what people are saying about him; that will immediately take his mind off your troubles.

Edgar Watson Howe

Never tell evil of a man if you do not know it for a certainty, and if you know it for a certainty, then ask yourself, "Why should I tell it?"

Jonathan K. Lavater

If you say of a rabbi that he does not have a good voice and of a cantor that he is not a scholar, you are a gossip. But if you say of a rabbi that he is no scholar and of a cantor that he has no voice – you are a murderer.

Rabbi Israel Salanter

Speak not all you think. Thoughts are your own; your words are so no more.

Patrick Delaney

The vanity of being trusted with a secret is generally one of the chief motives to disclose it.

Samuel Johnson

Have you heard something? Let it die with you. Be strong; it will not burst you.

Apocrypha
(Ecclesiasticus, 19:10)

Don't talk about yourself, it will be done when you leave.

Addison Mizner

INSULTS AND CRITICISMS

Political

The policeman and the trashman may call me Alice. You cannot.
Alice Roosevelt Longworth
(responding to the informality
of Sen. Joseph McCarthy)

Longworth's statement illustrates the hostility that even many anti-communists felt towards McCarthy for his role in *discrediting* anti-communism. As Ralph Flanders declared in the U.S. Senate in 1954, "Were the junior senator from Wisconsin in the pay of the Communists, he could not have done a better job for them." To this day, to call someone an anti-communist is to make him sound either like a warmonger or maniacal – in large measure a result of the irresponsibilities, exaggerations, and lies of Joseph McCarthy. During the Senator's heyday in the early 1950s, journalists Joseph and Stewart Alsop wrote: "McCarthy is the only major politician in the country who can be labeled 'liar' without fear of libel."

Other victims of Alice Roosevelt Longworth's sharp tongue were not always as deserving as McCarthy. The needlepoint inscription that this feisty daughter of President Theodore Roosevelt kept in her sitting room speaks for itself: "If you haven't got anything good to say about someone, come and sit by me."

He is an immortal. He has no heart, no brain, no guts. How can a man like that die?

George Clemenceau
(on Henri Petain, Commander in
Chief of France's army during
World War I, who became a
Nazi collaborator in World War II)

When I am right I get angry. Churchill gets angry when he is wrong. So we were very often angry at each other.

Charles de Gaulle

Winston Churchill always maintained that de Gaulle's hostility toward him and England was purely psychological: "England's grievous offense in de Gaulle's eyes is that she has helped France. He cannot bear to think that she needed help."

As they say, and aptly, "No good deed goes unpunished."

Lady Astor: If you were my husband I'd poison your tea.
Winston Churchill: If you were my wife, I'd drink it.

I had always cherished the above exchange, both because of my admiration for Churchill and my distaste for the bigoted Member of Parliament, Lady Astor. But, to my chagrin, Martin Gilbert, Churchill's official biographer, recently informed me that the episode is definitely apocryphal. He consoled me with a different exchange, this one, fortunately, authentic: George Bernard Shaw sent Churchill two tickets for the opening night of a new play, "One for you, and bring a friend, if you have one." Churchill responded, "I am busy opening night. Please send me two tickets for the second performance, if there is one."

Lady Astor was herself rarely bested in verbal battles. When a heckler interrupted a campaign speech with the cry, "Your husband's a millionaire, isn't he?" she replied: "I hope so. That's why I married him."

Jerry Ford is a nice guy, but he played too much football with his helmet off.

President Lyndon Johnson

President Johnson's contempt for Ford's naïve unworldliness was probably fed by one incident in particular. Speaker of the House John McCormack said to Ford, then the House minority leader, "The President said to be sure to see the Pagodas when you visit China." Ford responded: "Tell him I'm going to make every effort to have dinner with them." (This was quoted by Johnson's former assistant, Bill Moyers, on "The David Susskind Show," in October, 1974.)

An infamous quote of Ford's, which was much more significant, may well have cost him the presidency in 1976. During a debate with Jimmy Carter, Ford, perhaps hoping to appeal to the pride of Americans of Eastern European ancestry, declared: "There is no Soviet domination of Eastern Europe." Ford's other slips have generally been innocuous. For example: "If Lincoln were alive today, he'd roll over in his grave."

The greatest man who ever came out of Plymouth Corner, Vermont.

Clarence Darrow
(on President Calvin Coolidge)

The most analytical statement made by Thomas E. Dewey during the 1948 campaign was, "Ladies and gentlemen, the future lies before us."

William F. Buckley, Jr.
(mocking the Republican
presidential candidate)
This was quoted in Jeffrey Hart's
When the Going Was Good.
Buckley is definitely not the
best person to antagonize.
When a certain Dr. Prickman
sent him an abusive letter, Buckley
responded, "My friends call me Buck.
What do your friends call you?"

Fortunately, political criticism can be a little more gentle . . .

Hubert Humphrey talks so fast that listening to him is like trying to read *Playboy* with your wife turning the pages.

Sen. Barry Goldwater

And in England, political invective is often more stinging (and dryer) than in the United States . . .

If a traveller were informed that such a man [Lord John Russell] was the leader of the House of Commons, he might begin to comprehend how the Egyptians worshipped an insect.

Benjamin Disraeli
(quoted in Nancy McPhee's
The Book of Insults)

He made his conscience not his guide, but his accomplice.

Benjamin Disraeli
(on William Gladstone)

On another occasion, **Disraeli** carefully used the phrase "a misfortune and a calamity," and was asked to differentiate between the two: "If Gladstone fell into the Thames that would be a misfortune, and if anybody pulled him out, that, I suppose, would be a calamity."

He could never see a belt without hitting below it.

Margot Asquith
(wife of British prime minister Herbert
Asquith, on David Lloyd George)

The only recorded instance in history of a rat swimming toward a sinking ship.

Winston Churchill
(referring to a Tory who had
defected to the Liberals)
In the early 1970s,
Eugene McCarthy used the
same imagery to describe
Gov. John Connelly's move
to the Republican Party.

The Arts

As an artist I take my hat off to you. As a man I put it back on.

Arturo Toscanini
(to Richard Strauss)
Toscanini had refused to conduct
Wagner's *Parsifal* at the Beyreuth
Festival after the Nazi takeover of
Germany. Strauss replaced him and
became the Nazis' favorite conductor.

Most of the following attacks were so widely applicable that the victims have mercifully been forgotten.

Very nice though there are dull stretches.

Antoine de Rivarol
(1753 – 1801)
(reacting to a two-line poem)

Your manuscript is both good and original, but the part that is good is not original, and the part that is original is not good.

Samuel Johnson

This novel is not to be tossed aside lightly, but to be thrown with great force.

Dorothy Parker

There was laughter in the back of the theater, leading to the belief that someone was telling jokes back there.

George S. Kaufman

It was one of those plays in which all the actors unfortunately enunciated very clearly.

Robert Benchley

They shoot too many pictures and not enough actors.

Walter Winchell

Movie director **Alfred Hitchcock** was also reputed to be hostile to actors, although he always denied making the statement commonly attributed to him: "Actors are like cattle." "What I said was, 'All actors should be treated like cattle'."

Miscellaneous

The next time anyone asks you, "What is Bertrand Russell's philosophy?" the correct answer is "What year please?"

Sidney Hook

He's a great writer but I wouldn't want to shake his hand.

Jacqueline Susann
(on Philip Roth's
Portnoy's Complaint)

She was reacting to the
major activity engaged in by
Roth's protagonist: masturbation.

The only reason so many people showed up was to make sure
that he was dead.
Samuel Goldwyn
(speaking of producer
Louis B. Mayer's funeral)

A year later, in 1958, comedian **Red Skelton** commented on the
crowds at producer Harry Cohn's funeral: "It proves what they
always say; give the public what they want to see and they'll come
out for it."

We cannot put the face of a person on a stamp unless said person
is deceased. My suggestion therefore is that you drop dead.
Postmaster General
James Edward Day
(to a correspondent who had
demanded to be portrayed
on a U.S. postage stamp)

When God wants to punish a joke he sends it to your grandmother.
Grandfather of acquaintance
(elaborating on his wife's unique
ability to ruin punch lines)

Some people are so open-minded that their brains fall out.
Lionel Trilling

COMPLIMENTS

It would be nice if sometimes the kind things I say were considered worthy of quotation. It isn't difficult, you know, to be witty or amusing when one has something to say that is destructive, but damned hard to be clever and quotable when you are singing someone's praises.

Noel Coward

Political

Do you remember that in classical times when Cicero finished speaking, the people said, "How well he spoke!" – but when Demosthenes had finished speaking, the people said, "Let us march."

Adlai Stevenson
(in 1960, ruefully contrasting
John F. Kennedy's charisma
with his own appeal)

She would rather light a candle than curse the darkness, and her glow has warmed the world.

Adlai Stevenson
(eulogizing Eleanor Roosevelt, 1962)

I succeed him: no one can replace him.

Thomas Jefferson
This was Jefferson's response
when he arrived as the new
U.S. ambassador to France
in 1785 and was asked,
"Is it you, Sir, who replaces
Dr. [Benjamin] Franklin?"

I think this is the most extraordinary collection of talent and of
human knowledge that has ever been gathered together at the
White House – with the possible exception of when Thomas
Jefferson dined alone.

John F. Kennedy
(at a White House reception for
fifty-one U.S. Nobel Prize winners)

In the dark days and darker nights when England stood alone –
and most men save Englishmen despaired of England's life – he
mobilized the English language and sent it into battle.

John F. Kennedy
(conferring honorary citizenship
on Winston Churchill in 1961)
Churchill was the first
person so honored.

If I knew what brand he drinks, I would send a barrel or so to my
other generals.

Abraham Lincoln
(responding to a complaint about
Gen. Ulysses S. Grant's drinking habits)

You are better off than I am, for while you have lost only your left, I have lost my right arm.

> **Robert E. Lee**
> (quoted in Miriam Ringo's
> book *Nobody Said It Better*)
> Lee's words were written
> in an 1863 letter to Gen.
> Thomas "Stonewall" Jackson
> after Jackson was accidentally
> shot by his own men and lost his
> left arm. Six days later he died.

He rose without a friend and sat down without an enemy.

> **Henry Gratten**
> (on speech of Charles Lucas
> to the Irish parliament)

The Arts, Philosophy, Religion and Love

When God made Carl, he didn't do anything else that day.

> **Edward Steichen**
> (on poet Carl Sandburg)

I am not an orphan on earth as long as this man is alive.

> **Maxim Gorky**
> (on Leo Tolstoy)

I have never but once succeeded in making him [George Edward Moore] tell a lie, and that was by a subterfuge.

"Moore," I said, "Do you always tell the truth?"

"No," he replied.

I believe this to be the only lie he ever told.

Bertrand Russell
(Autobiography)

When at length he came to die he left only a knife, a fork, two spoons and the Methodist Church.

Anonymous obituary
for John Wesley
(eighteenth-century founder
of the Methodist Church)

The following rather elaborate Talmudic blessing is often adapted and recited at Jewish weddings:

Rabbi Nahman once asked **Rabbi Isaac** to bless him as they were saying goodbye. Rabbi Isaac replied: "Let me give you a parable. A man traveled a long way in the desert. He felt hungry, weary and thirsty, when suddenly he came upon a tree filled with sweet fruits, covered with branches that provided shade, and watered by a brook that flowed nearby. The man rested in the tree's shade, ate of its fruits and drank its water. When he was about to leave he turned to the tree and said: 'O tree, beautiful tree, how shall I bless you? Shall I wish that your shade be pleasant? It is already pleasant. Shall I say that your fruits should be sweet? They are sweet. Shall I ask that a brook flow by you? A brook does flow by you. Therefore, I will bless you this way: May it be God's will that all the shoots taken from you be just like you.'

"So it is with you," Rabbi Isaac said to Rabbi Nahman. "What can I wish you? Shall I wish you learning? You have learning. Wealth? You have wealth. Children? You have children. Therefore I say: May it be God's will that all your offspring be like you."

Talmud
(Tractate *Taanith* 5b-6a,
translated by Francine Klagsbrun,
in her book *Voices of Wisdom*)

If I can't be who I am, who would I most like to be? Lady Churchill's second husband.

Winston Churchill,
at a banquet where each
speaker was asked the question:
"If you couldn't be who you are,
who would you like to be?"

GOOD ADVICE

On Giving Advice: When you can, always advise people to do what they really want to do.... Doing what they want to do, they may succeed; doing what they don't want to do, they won't.
James Gould Cozzens

Arguing: The best way I know of to win an argument is to start by being in the right.
Lord Hailsham

Books: I never lend books, for no one ever returns them; the only books I have in my library are books that other folks have lent me.
Anatole France

Commitment: If you start to take Vienna – take Vienna.
Napoleon Bonaparte
(cited in preface to William Safire and
Leonard Safire's book *Good Advice)*

William Safire remarks that the above is his favorite quotation: "There's a verb in that quote that shows the way. Not a lot of talk about the need to follow through on a commitment, or about the dangers of appearing indecisive, but a pristine point – 'take Vienna.' Once you have tossed your hat over the wall, climb the wall; don't turn back. That's good advice."

Confession: Confession may be good for one's own soul, but our obligation extends to the other person's soul as well. And confession of our sins to another can sometimes be terrible for that person's soul.

Joseph Telushkin

A Jewish joke tells of a man pacing his bedroom floor at three o'clock in the morning. His wife wakes up and asks him why he can't sleep. "You know Sam, our next-door neighbor? I owe him $1,000 – due tomorow – and I don't have it."

His wife gets up and opens the window. "Sam," she yells. And then again and again – "Sam! Sam!" Finally a very tired man comes to the window.

"What is it?"

"You know the $1,000 my husband owes you? He doesn't have it." She slams the window shut and turns to her husband.

"Now, *you* sleep, and let *him* pace the floor."

My skepticism about the value of confessing all of one's sins to another is confirmed by a passage in **W. Somerset Maugham**'s diary, *A Writer's Notebook:*

"He was a successful lawyer, and it was a shock to his family and his friends when he committed suicide. He was a breezy, energetic, exuberant man, and the last person you would have expected to do away with himself. He enjoyed life. His origins were humble, but for his services in the war he had been granted a baronetcy. He adored his only son, who would succeed to his title, follow him into the business, go into Parliament and make a name for himself. No one could guess why he had killed himself.

He had arranged it so that it should look like an accident, and so it would have been considered except for a small oversight on his part. It was true that his wife was causing him a certain amount of anxiety. . . . She was not mad enough to be put in an asylum, but certainly not sane. She suffered from severe melancholia. They didn't tell her that her husband had committed suicide, but only that he had been killed in a motor accident. She took it better than was expected. It was her doctor who broke the news to her. 'Thank God I told him when I did,' she said. 'If I hadn't I should never have had another moment's peace in my life.' The doctor wanted to know what she meant. After a while she told him: she had confessed to her husband that the son he doted on, the son on whom all his hopes were set, was not his."

Courage: Tell a man he's brave and you help him to become so.

Carlyle

Cowardice: It is better to be a coward for a minute than dead for the rest of your life.

Irish proverb

Decision-Making: When against one's will one is high-pressured into making a hurried decision, the best answer is always "No" because "No" is more easily changed to "Yes" than "Yes" is changed to "No."

Charles Wilson

Economics: When Nobel Prize-winning economist **Milton Friedman** served as adviser to Israeli Prime Minister Menachem Begin, he delivered a speech on economics to the Knesset. After his speech, Shlomo Lorincz, a Knesset member, said to him, "In the Talmud, Hillel summarized Judaism in one sentence: 'What is hateful unto you, don't do unto your neighbor; the rest is commentary.' Could you summarize economics in one sentence?"

"Yes," replied Friedman. "There is no such thing as a free lunch."

Ego: No one can make you feel inferior without your consent.

Eleanor Roosevelt

Gambling: It may be that the race is not always to the swift nor the battle to the strong – but that's the way to bet.

Damon Runyon

One of these days in your travels a guy is going to come up to you and show you a nice brand-new deck of cards on which the seal is not yet broken, and this guy is going to offer to bet you that he can make the jack of spades jump out of the deck and squirt cider in your ear. But, son, do not bet this man, for as sure as you stand here, you are going to wind up with an earful of cider.

Damon Runyon

Goodness: Judge men not by their opinions, but by what their opinions have made of them.

Georg Lichtenberg

Few religious groups in the United States hold beliefs as seemingly untenable to the rest of the society as the Mormons. Yet the life style that they lead in Utah, in terms of charitableness, material success and family cohesiveness, is far from unimpressive.

George Will noted that "the Mormon sensibility sometimes makes Utah seem to others like an enclave surrounded on four sides by reality. Certainly a different reality is just an hour's flight away, in Denver, where a nightclub advertises: THE NEWEST ENTERTAINMENT RAGE – MUD WRESTLING. BEAUTIFUL GIRLS FIGHTING TOPLESS IN A PIT OF REAL MUD. Some people evidently think that it matters that the mud is 'real.' And these people probably think Mormons are peculiar" (syndicated column, January 21, 1979).

It is better for my enemy to see good in me than for me to see evil in him.

Yiddish proverb

Humorous Advice: Do not join encounter groups. If you enjoy being made to feel inadequate, call your mother.

Liz Smith

You can get a lot more done with a kind word and a gun, than with a kind word alone.

Al Capone
(quoted by economist Walter Heller
on wage and price control legislation)

Never go to a doctor whose office plants have died.

Erma Bombeck

We should forgive our enemies, but only after they have been hanged first.

Heinrich Heine

Buy old masters. They fetch better prices than old mistresses.

Lord Beaverbrook

Jealousy: A man must be always considerate of the feelings of his neighbors. . . . So, for instance, if I went out to the fair. . . and did well, sold everything at a good profit, and returned with pockets full of money. . . I never failed to tell my neighbors that I had lost every cent and was a ruined man. Thus, I was happy and my neighbors were happy. But if, on the contrary, I had really been cleaned out at the fair. . . I made sure to tell my neighbors that never since God made fairs had there been a better one. You get my point? For thus I was miserable and my neighbors were miserable.

Sholom Aleichem
(quoted in Francine Klagsbrun's
book *Voices of Wisdom*)

Joy: The best way to cheer yourself up is to try and cheer somebody else up.

Mark Twain

Love: Don't give to lovers you will replace irreplaceable presents.

Logan Pearsall Smith

Never go to bed mad. Stay up and fight.

Phyllis Diller
(Phyllis Diller's Housekeeping Hints)

Marriage: Only choose in marriage a woman whom you would choose as a friend if she were a man.

Joseph Joubert

Public Speaking: If after twenty minutes you don't strike oil, stop boring.

Rabbi Joseph Lookstein
(to homiletics class at
Yeshiva University, New York)

Self-Confidence: If you do not believe in yourself, do not blame others for lacking faith in you.

Brendan Francis

Self-Improvement: First improve yourself, then improve others.

Talmud
(Tractate Bava Mezia, 107b)

If you won't be better tomorrow than you were today, then what do you need tomorrow for?

Rabbi Nahman of Bratslav

Simplicity: Everything should be made as simple as possible – but not simpler.

Albert Einstein

Stock Market: Don't try to buy at the bottom and sell at the top. This can't be done – except by liars.

Bernard Baruch

Success: If you would be remembered, do one thing superbly well.

Saunders Norvell

Worry: **Rabbi Yehiel** maintained that he had learnt from his teachers never to worry about two things – what can be corrected and what cannot be corrected. What can be corrected should be corrected at once, without any worry. And as for what cannot be corrected, worrying will not help.

Rabbi Shmuel Avidor Ha-Cohen
(Touching Heaven, Touching Earth)

BETWEEN MAN AND GOD

GOD

Faith And Doubt

If only God would give me some clear sign! Like making a large deposit in my name at a Swiss bank.

Woody Allen

God may have His own reasons for denying us certainty with regard to His existence and nature. One reason apparent to us is that man's certainty with regard to anything is poison to his soul. Who knows this better than moderns who have had to cope with dogmatic Fascists, Communists and even scientists.

Emmanuel Rackman
(The Condition of Jewish Belief)

If I knew Him I'd be Him.

Medieval Jewish proverb

Many today have doubts about God's existence, but they live as if God does not exist. They are agnostics, but live as atheists. . . . You may be agnostic in theory, but in practice you live either a religious or a secular life.

**Dennis Prager and
Joseph Telushkin**
*(The Nine Questions
People Ask About Judaism)*

Nobody can believe all the time. What you must do is accept your moods of doubt. . . . You must say to yourself: "Here I am, a believer who is doubting."

Louis Auchincloss
(The Rector of Justin)

Experience has repeatedly confirmed that well-known maxim of Bacon's that "a little philosophy inclineth a man's mind to atheism, but depth in philosophy bringeth men's minds about to religion. . . ." When Bacon penned the sage epigram. . . he forgot to add that the God to whom depth in philosophy brings back men's minds is far from being the same from whom a little philosophy estranges them.

George Santayana

Where there is the necessary technical skill to move mountains there is no need for the faith that moves mountains.

Eric Hoffer
(The Passionate State of Mind)

Perhaps the main reason doctors are so highly venerated in the modern world is because of their expertise in areas once thought to be the exclusive province of God. Two hundred years ago, if a woman could not conceive, she beseeched God through prayer. In a similar situation today, prayers may still be offered, but even religious people are apt to rely more heavily on the gynecologist's treatment.

In the final analysis, for the believer there are no questions, and for the non-believer there are no answers.

Haffetz Hayyim
(Polish rabbi)

Loving And Fighting With God

In **Isaac Bashevis Singer**'s novel, *The Slave,* Jacob, a deeply religious man whose family has been murdered by antisemites, ruminates: "I have no doubt that you are the Almighty and that whatever you do is for the best, but it is impossible for me to obey the commandment, 'You shall love your God.' No. I cannot, Father, not in this life."

The knowledge of God is very far from the love of Him.

Blaise Pascal
(Pensées)

Do not think you can frighten me by telling me that I am alone. France is alone; and God is alone; and what is my loneliness before the loneliness of my country and my God?

Saint Joan
(in George Bernard Shaw's
St. Joan)

In recent years, a theologian in Israel, **David Hartman,** has argued that the one truly tragic figure in the Bibls is God, because His expectations are constantly disappointed.

The Jew may love God, or he may fight with God, but he may not ignore God.

Elie Wiesel

Wiesel, the best-known writer on the Holocaust, is also the most famous fighter with God of this generation. In assuming this role he stands in a long Jewish tradition, in which it is the believers who express their anger and disappointment, as well as their love, to God. This possibly unique tradition goes back to biblical figures. The prophet Habakkuk laments, "How long, O Lord, shall I cry out and You not listen?" (Habakkuk 1:2). The Psalmist demands of God, "Awake, why do you sleep. O Lord.... Why do You hide Your face, and forget our suffering and oppression?" (Psalms 44:24-5). And in a stark passage in Job, "From out of the city the dying groan, and the soul of the wounded cry for help; yet God pays no attention to their prayers" (Job 24:12).

Hundreds of years later, the **Talmud** recorded the reaction of the school of Rabbi Ishmael to God's inaction while the Romans destroyed Jerusalem: "Who is like You among the dumb?" (Gittin 56b). During the Holocaust a story was told of a rabbi in a concentration camp who said to his followers, "There is a possibility that God is a liar." His disciples, shocked at the blasphemy, demanded that he explain himself. "Because when God looks down at Auschwitz, He says 'I am not responsible for this.' And that is a lie."

The anger in all these cases stems from the belief that God has responsibilities, just as man does, and is to be criticized when He fails to fulfill them. This challenging attitude goes back to Abraham who questioned God: "Shall not the judge of all the earth act with justice?" (Genesis 18:25). A striking feature in all these examples is the intimate relationship these believers had with God.

Questions About Christianity

Can you imagine our Savior dying for all of us, yet we have to argue over whether He didn't die for us personally and not for you. Sometimes you wonder if His lesson of sacrifice and devotion was pretty near lost on a lot of us.

Will Rogers

The basis of your religion is injustice: the Son of God, the pure, the immaculate, the innocent, is sacrificed for the guilty.

Lord Byron

Christ died for our sins. Dare we make his martyrdom meaningless by not committing them?

Jules Feiffer
(quoted in Laurence S. Peter's
Peter's Quotations)

Feiffer has touched on what is, for non-Christians, the most inexplicable aspect of Christianity: the belief that Jesus' crucifixion brings Christians forgiveness even for sins committed against others. Martin Luther was so adamant that the only issue in salvation is faith in Jesus' martyrdom, that he wrote: "It is sufficient that we recognize...the lamb who bears the sins of the world; from this, sin does not sever us, even if thousands, thousands of times in one day we should fornicate or murder" (in a letter to Philip Melanchthon, August 1, 1521).

By emphasizing faith and not deeds, Luther disregarded the Hebrew biblical tradition. Walter Kauffman suggests that he uses even the New Testament traditions selectively: "Since James, Jesus' brother, says in his Epistle, 'Faith without good deeds is useless' (James 2:20) Luther says that this Epistle is 'utter straw'" (Luther quotations, Walter Kaufmann, *Religions in Four Dimensions*).

One may say with one's lips: I believe that God is one, and also three – but no one can believe it, because the words have no sense.

Leo Tolstoy
(What is Religion)

Christianity has not been tried and found wanting: it has been found difficult and not tried.

G. K. Chesterton

Most people really believe that the Christian commandments (e.g. love one's neighbor as oneself) are intentionally a little too severe – like putting the clock ahead half an hour to make sure of not being late in the morning.

Søren Kierkegaard

If Jesus Christ were to come today, people would not even crucify him. They would ask him to dinner, hear what he had to say, and make fun of it.

Thomas Carlyle

Man's Misuse Of God

What mean and cruel things men do for the love of God.

> **W. Somerset Maugham**
> *(A Writer's Notebook)*
> The biblical depiction of the ancient
> Canaanites tells: "They burned their
> sons and daughters in fires as offerings
> to their gods" [Deuteronomy 12:31].

The Crusaders are probably the most notorious example of murderers acting for the "love" of God. In 1209, for example, a Crusader army defeated the French city of Beziers, which contained, according to a bishop's report, 220 Christian heretics, known as Cathars. Unable to ferret out the heretics, the Crusaders asked the papal commander Arnaud Amalric, "Lord, what shall we do! We cannot distinguish the good from the wicked." Pope Innocent III's representative ruled: "Kill them all. God will recognize His own." Fifteen thousand people were murdered in one day. The Pope promised the Crusaders forgiveness of all sins, and safety from all creditors (Otto Friedrich, *The End of the World*).

Every man thinks God is on his side.

> **Jean Anouilh**
> *(The Lark)*

The third of the Ten Commandments, "You shall not take God's name in vain," is usually misunderstood to mean that it is blasphemous to say words such as goddamn. Many are puzzled that such an act is listed in the document that forbids murdering, stealing, idolatry and adultery. However, "You shall not take God's name in vain" is a misleading translation of the Hebrew, which literally means "You shall not carry God's name in vain"; in other words, don't use God as your justification in selfish causes.

The Third Commandment is the only one of the ten concerning which God says, "for the Lord God will not forgive him who carries His name in vain" (Exodus 20:6-7). The reason is now clear. When a person commits an evil act, he discredits himself. But when a religious person commits an evil act in the name of God, he discredits God. As a result, God pronounces this sin unpardonable.

To maintain that our successes are due to Providence and not to our own cleverness, is a cunning way of increasing in our own eyes the importance of our successes.

Cesare Pavese

If God made man in His image we have certainly returned the compliment.

Voltaire

God And Good

"Where is the dwelling of God?" This is the question with which the **Rabbi of Kotzk** surprised a number of learned men who happened to be visiting him. They laughed at him: "What a thing to ask! Is not the whole world full of His glory?" Then he answered his own question: "God dwells wherever man lets Him in."

Martin Buber
(Tales of the Hasidim – Later Masters)

What does the Lord require of you? To do justice, love goodness and walk modestly with your God.

Micah 6:8

Most would have difficulty in describing what God wants of man in as clear and ethical terms as this Hebrew prophet did 2,700 years ago. Perhaps Micah's stark clarity makes him seem simplistic while his ethical requirements make him seem too demanding.

He who truly fears a thing flees from it, but he who truly fears God, flees unto Him.

Al-Qushayri

God has not called me to be successful; he has called me to be faithful.

Mother Teresa of Calcutta

Anti-God

The fact that a believer is happier than a skeptic is no more to the point than the fact that a drunken man is happier than a sober one.

George Bernard Shaw

It takes a long while for a naturally trustful person to reconcile himself to the idea that after all God will not help him.

H. L. Mencken

The only excuse for God is that He doesn't exist.

Stendahl

I do not pretend to be able to prove that there is no God. I equally cannot prove that Satan is a fiction. The Christian God may exist; so may the gods of Olympus or of ancient Egypt or of Babylon. But not one of these hypotheses is more probable than any other.

Bertrand Russell
(What I Believe)

We only speak of faith when we wish to substitute emotion for evidence. We are told that faith could remove mountains, but no one believed it. We are now told that the atomic bomb can remove mountains and everyone believes it.

Bertrand Russell
*(Human Society in
Ethics and Politics)*

God is always on the side which has the best football coach.

Heywood Hale Broun

God needs immortality to vindicate His ways to man.

W. Somerset Maugham
(The Summing Up)

I have left out of this section personal vendettas, for example, Lenin's "I hate God as I do my personal enemies" *(New Life,* December 16, 1905), since it reveals a great deal about Lenin and nothing about God.

Miscellaneous

I fear God and next to God I chiefly fear him who fears Him not.
Moslih Eddin Saadi
(thirteenth-century intellect)

God made everything out of nothing. But the nothingness shows through.

Paul Valéry

If there be a God, the Cardinal will have much for which to answer. If there be none, he will have lived a successful life.
Pope Urban VIII
(on the death of Cardinal
Richelieu, the seventeenth-
century churchman and
Chief Minister of Louis XIII)

If I had believed in a God of reward and punishments, I might have lost courage in battle.

Napoleon Bonaparte
(to Gaspard Gourgard
at St. Helena)

A God all mercy is a God unjust.

Edward Young

IS GOD NECESSARY FOR MORALITY?

If there is no God, all is permitted.

Ivan Karamazov,
in Feodor Dostoevsky's
The Brothers Karamazov.

In the nineteenth century the problem was that God was dead; in the twentieth century the problem is that man is dead.

Erich Fromm
(The Sane Society)

Although a favorite argument of secular humanists against religion is that many evils have been perpetrated in its name, it is seldom noted that the two most murderous societies in history – the Bolsheviks and the Nazis – were aggressively atheistic. Hitler declared his mission in life to be the destruction of the "tyrannical God of the Jews"; and in the Soviet Union it is a crime to advocate belief in God.

The above quote from Dostoevsky is often cited as a prophecy of the horrors of the twentieth century. But more likely, Dostoevsky was just stating a logical conclusion – if there is no God, then who is to say that everything should not be permitted? To this day there is ultimately no real answer to the question, "Why was Hitler wrong?" aside from "Because God said so." The perplexity into which this thrusts moral atheists was perfectly articulated by the most prominent secular philosopher of this century, **Bertrand Russell.** "I cannot see how to refute the arguments for the subjectivity of ethical values, but I find myself incapable of believing that all that is wrong with wanton cruelty is that I don't like it."

Though Russell lived well into his nineties, he was never able to produce a stronger argument against wanton cruelty than that he didn't like it. Unfortunately, a considerable number of people do like it. And, ironically, moral atheists have themselves helped lay the philosophical basis for those who like it.

"Bad" people like Hitler and Goering simply carried out more or less consistently many of the ideas long held by respectable "good" people. . . . How do good people deny morality? In many ways:

"I believe in morals but all morals are relative."

"I have my own private code."

"Morals are entirely a matter of opinion."

"There are no absolutes in morals that can rationally be discovered."

A Hitler or Mussolini could accept every one of these statements.

Oliver Martin
(Two Educators)

Should that most unshaken rule of morality and foundation of all social virtue, "that one should do as he would be done unto," be proposed to one who had never heard of it before . . . might he not without any absurdity ask a reason why?

John Locke
(Essay Concerning Human Understanding, 1890)

Secular humanists, responding to Locke's challenge, usually claim that reason and education can bring about a universally observed morality. A renowned philosopher at Yale University, Brand Blanshard, wrote: "Rationality, or the attempt at it, takes the place of faith. . . . Take reason seriously. . . . Let it shape belief and conduct freely. It will shape them aright if anything can" (*The Humanist*, November-December, 1974). Sigmund Freud, a humanist, though no optimist about human nature, placed great faith in secular education. Writing in Vienna in 1927, he declared: "Civilization has little to fear from educated people and brain-workers. In them the replacement of religious motives for civilized behavior by other secular motives would proceed unobtrusively" (*The Future of An Illusion*). Less than ten years after he made this statement, the Nazis had occupied Austria, and Freud witnessed his fellow intellectuals showing no more moral strength than any other group in Austria and Germany. Many intellectuals actually supported Nazism, and as Max Weinreich's *Hitler's Professors* documents, quite a number participated in its atrocities.

At the same time, in other parts of the Western world, many prominent intellectuals supported Stalin's murderous regime. Clearly, though reason and education can bring about much good, they are, in and of themselves, amoral.

The use of reason to justify what is wrong is so common that we have a special word for it – rationalization.

Dennis Prager and Joseph Telushkin
(The Nine Questions People Ask About Judaism)

If men are so wicked with religion, what would they be without it?

Benjamin Franklin

Can one be a saint without God? That's the problem, in fact the only problem, I'm up against today.

Albert Camus
(The Plague)

PRAYER

On The Misuse Of Prayer

Every prayer reduces itself to this: Great God, grant that two plus two not equal four.

Ivan Turgenev
(Prayer)

There are few men who dare to publish to the world the prayers they make to Almighty God.

Montaigne

In 1863, **Abraham Lincoln** said to Rev. Byron Sunderland, Chaplain of the Senate: "We on our side are praying Him to give us victory because we believe we are right; but those on the other side pray to Him too, for victory, believing they are right. What must He think of us?"

The notion of offering prayers for success in war so irritated **Mark Twain** that he composed this ultimate war prayer: "O Lord our God, help us to tear their soldiers to bloody shreds with our shells...help us to drown the thunder of the guns with the shrieks of their wounded...help us lay waste their humble bones...help us to wring the hearts of their unoffending widows with unavailing grief.... We ask it, in the spirit of love of Him who is the Source of Love and who is the ever-faithful refuge and friend of all that are beset and seek His aid with humble and contrite hearts. Amen" (published posthumously in *Europe and Elsewhere*).

In the early 1700s, as Queen Caroline of England lay dying, Princess Emily requested the Archbishop of Canterbury to pray. **Sir Robert Walpole,** the Prime Minister, responded: "Let this farce be played. . . . It will do the Queen no hurt, no more than any good, and it will satisfy all the wise and good fools, who will call us all atheists if we don't pretend to be as great fools as they are."

Two things are striking in Walpole's statement: the surprising bluntness about popular religiosity in an eighteenth-century English court, and, that though Walpole was not an atheist, people would regard him as such if he did not pray for a miracle.

Purpose Of Prayer

Prayer does not change God, but it changes him who prays.
                                                    Søren Kierkegaard

The Hebrew word for prayer, *l'hitpallel,* is a *reflexive* verb meaning "to judge or to examine oneself." God does not need our prayers, we do. A person who takes time out regularly to examine himself is inevitably affected by the act.

When the children of Israel came to the Red Sea and Moses prayed a long time, God said to him: "My children are in trouble, the sea before them, and the enemy behind them, why do you stand here indulging in long prayers?"
                                            Rabbi Eliezer ben Hyrcanus
                                                (first-century rabbi, in
                                            commentary on Exodus 14:15)

William Penn took a friend to a Quaker service. After an hour of silence the friend asked Penn, "When does the service begin?" Penn responded, "The service begins when the meeting ends."

James Hume
(Roles Speakers Play)

Pray as if everything depended on God and work as if everything depended on man.

Francis Cardinal Spellman

God, You help complete strangers, so why don't You help me?

Anonymous Yiddish prayer

SIN AND REPENTANCE

It is much easier to repent of sins that we have committed than to repent of those we intend to commit.

Josh Billings

If a man has beheld evil, he may know that it was shown to him in order that he learn his own guilt and repent; for what is shown to him is also within him.

Rabbi Israel Baal Shem Tov

We confess our faults in the plural, and deny them in the singular.

Richard Fulke Greville
(Maxims, Characters and Reflections)

Rabbi Bunam of Pzysha once asked his disciples, "How can you tell when a sin you have committed has been pardoned?" His disciples gave various answers but none of them pleased the rabbi. "We can tell," he said, "by the fact that we no longer commit that sin."

Martin Buber
(Tales of the Hasidim – Later Masters)

To abstain from sin when a man cannot sin is to be forsaken by sin, not to forsake it.

Saint Augustine

All human sin seems so much worse in its consequence than in its intentions.

Reinhold Niebuhr
*(Leaves From the
Notebook of a Tamed Cynic)*

My hope is that you don't sin, not because it is forbidden, but because there isn't enough time.
Rabbi Menahem Mendl of Kotzk

How immense appear to us the sins we have not committed.
Madame Necker

When **Calvin Coolidge** returned from Church one Sunday his wife asked him what the minister had spoken about.

"Sin," the taciturn Coolidge responded.

"And what did he say?" his wife asked.

"He was against it."

ORGANIZED RELIGION

Religious Tolerance

Every sect is a moral check on its neighbor. Competition is as wholesome in religion as in commerce.

W. S. Landor
(Imaginary Conversations, 1824;
quoted in H. L. Mencken's
A New Dictionary of Quotations)

Landor's statement has proved prophetic, at least with regard to America. The multitude of religions in the United States has forced most of them to become far more tolerant than they were in those countries where they were the dominant religion. Catholicism in America, for example, has generally been much more open towards non-Catholics than Catholicism in France, Italy or Ireland.

Compulsion in religion is distinguished peculiarly from compulsion in every other thing. I may grow rich by an art I am compelled to follow; I may recover health by medicines I am compelled to take against my own judgment. But I cannot be saved by a worship I disbelieve and abhor.

Thomas Jefferson
(Notes on Religion)

We must accept the other fellow's religion . . . to the extent that we respect his theory that his wife is beautiful.

H. L. Mencken
(Minority Report)

He who steadily observes those moral precepts in which all religions concur, will never be questioned at the gates of heaven as to the dogmas in which they all differ.

Thomas Jefferson
(Letter to William Canby, 1813)

An **Anglican minister** and a **Catholic priest** were arguing about religion. Finally, one said to the other, "But after all, we each worship God, you in your way, I in His."

Attacks On Organized Religion

I think all the great religions of the world – Buddhism, Hinduism, Christianity, Islam, and Communism – both untrue and harmful. It is evident as a matter of logic that since they disagree, not more than one of them can be true. With very few exceptions, the religion which a man accepts is that of the community in which he lives, which makes it obvious that the influence of the environment is what has led him to accept the religion in question.

Bertrand Russell
(Why I Am Not A Christian)

A religion, even if it calls itself the religion of love, must be hard and unloving to those who do not belong to it. Fundamentally, every religion is a religion of love for those whom it embraces, while cruelty and intolerance towards those who do not belong to it are natural to every religion.

Sigmund Freud
*(Group Psychology and
an Analysis of the Ego)*

Because of Freud's stature in psychology, and because his antagonism to religion is so well known, many people have assumed that psychology and psychoanalysis are necessarily antagonistic to religion. However, **Carl Jung,** one of the most important psychoanalysts of this century, emphatically demonstrated that this need not be true: "I should like to call attention to the following facts. During the past thirty years, people from all civilized countries of the earth have consulted me. I have treated many hundreds of patients. . . Protestants. . . Jews [and a small number of Catholics]. Among all my patients. . . over thirty-five. . . there has not been one whose problem in the last resort was not that of finding a religious outlook on life. It is safe to say that every one of them fell ill because he had lost that which the living religions of every age have given to their followers, and none of them has really been healed who did not regain his religious outlook" *(Modern Man in Search of a Soul)*.

All the philosophers of the world who had a religion have said in all ages, "There is a God and one must be just." That, then, is the universal religion established in all ages and throughout mankind. The point in which they all agree is therefore true, and the systems through which they differ are therefore false.

Voltaire
(Philosophical Dictionary)

A man who should act for one day on the assumption that all the people about him were influenced by the religion which they professed, would find himself ruined before night.

T. B. Macaulay
(Civil Disabilities of the Jews)

The above sentiment is less a critique of religion than a condemnation of man's misuse and perversion of religion. As a general rule, it is the believers who are the most angered by the disparity between what their religion intended and how it is perverted.

Going to Church doesn't make you a Christian any more than going to a garage makes you an automobile.

Billy Sunday

Religion And Ethics

It is my duty not only to comfort the victims of the man who drives in a busy street like a menace, but also to try and stop him.

Dietrich Bonhoeffer
(Lutheran minister executed
by the Nazis for his involvement
in anti-Nazi activities)

The question of bread for myself is a material question, but the question of bread for my neighbor is a spiritual question.

Nikolai Berdyaev
(1874-1948)

Most people worry about their own financial needs and their neighbor's soul. Better that they should worry about their neighbor's financial needs and their own souls.

Rabbi Israel Salanter

It takes twice as much spiritual strength to be an honest businessman as to be an honest rabbi, but if you have that much spiritual strength why waste it on business?

Rabbi Israel Salanter
(to a student who felt
spiritually unworthy of
becoming a rabbi)

To test the worth of a man's religion, do business with him.

John Lancaster Spalding

It is a mistake to suppose that God is only, or even chiefly, concerned with religion.

William Temple
(Archbishop of Canterbury)

The tendency of religious people to define religiosity solely by ritual behavior is disturbing proof that they have accepted the secular world's definition of religion as something concerned only with man's relationship to God. As if the earliest religious writings of both Judaism and Christianity, the Hebrew Bible and the New Testament, did not stress ethics as God's central demand of man (see Micah 6:8). Jesus is similarly cited as understanding this to be the meaning of the Bible: "So always treat others as you would like them to treat you; that is the meaning of the Law and the Prophets" (Matthew 7:12, rephrasing the commandment "Love your neighbor as yourself" Leviticus 19:18).

Can Religion Be Rational?

Credo quia absurdum.
I believe because it is absurd.

Tertullian
(Church Father, circa 160-240)

Tertullian's sentiment is attractive to many religious and anti-religious people: to anti-religious people because it justifies dismissing religion as superstitious and contemptible, and to some religious people who fear that rational explanations of religious rituals and beliefs will make religion seem human rather than divine in origin. In the twelfth century, the greatest of all Jewish philosophers, **Moses Maimonides,** ridiculed Jews who opposed providing rational explanations for Jewish laws:

"For they think that if those laws were useful in this existence and had been given to us for this or that reason, it would be as if they derived from the reflection and understanding of some intelligent being. If, however, there is a thing for which the intellect could not find any meaning at all and that does not lead to something useful it indubitably derives from God: for the reflection of man would lead to no such thing" (*Guide to the Perplexed,* 3:31, translation of Shlomo Pines).

A carry-over of the Tertullian "absurdist" influence is discernible perhaps in the legal term "act of God," by which present-day courts designate actions that are capricious and destructive. The Tertullian mind-set is also present inside numerous cults, whose abilities to attract followers often increase the more anti-rational their beliefs. The Catholic Church rejected Tertullian's anti-rationalism, and there are few greater exponents of reason in religion than the seventeenth-century priest, Blaise Pascal, whose comments follow:

Men have contempt for religion. . . . To cure this it is necessary to begin by showing that religion is not contrary to reason; then that it is worthy of respect; next to make it loveable so that good men wish it were true and finally to show that it is true.

Blaise Pascal
(Pensées)

If we submit everything to reason, our religion will have nothing in it mysterious or supernatural. If we violate the principles of reason, our religion will be absurd and ridiculous.

Blaise Pascal
(Pensées)

Miscellaneous

A Unitarian is a person who believes there is, at most, one God.

Alfred North Whitehead

Buddhist scriptures contain the story of a man who once came to Gautama Buddha asking how he could obtain the secret of the meaning of religion. The founder of Buddhism seized the man and held his head under water. When he let the man up, gasping for breath, Buddha said to him: "When you want the meaning of religion as much as you wanted air, then you will find it."

Bernard Raskas
(Heart of Wisdom)

You have to be very religious to change your religion.

Comtesse Diane
(Maxims de la Vie)

A rabbi who they don't want to throw out of town is no rabbi, and a rabbi who lets himself be thrown out is no man.

Rabbi Israel Salanter

God has no religion.

Mahatma Gandhi
In William Shirer's *Gandhi —
A Memoir,* he quotes a similar
Gandhian sentiment: "I do not
believe that in the other world
there are either Hindus,
Christians, or Moslems."

The enormous fatigue of trying to live without religion.

Donald Barr
(Who Pushed Humpty Dumpty?)

Ronnie approved of religion as long as it endorsed the National Anthem, but he opposed it when it attempted to influence his life.

E. M. Forster
(A Passage to India)

The attempt to speak without speaking a specific language is not more hopeless than the attempt to have a religion that shall be no religion in particular.

George Santayana

Santayana's words apply with particular force to intermarrying couples who say they will raise their child with "religion," feeling no need to specify one or the other.

BETWEEN MAN AND HIMSELF

HUMAN NATURE – A SOMBER LOOK

Normal men have killed perhaps 100,000,000 of their fellow normal men in the last fifty years.

R. D. Laing
(The Politics of Experience)

Man is the only animal who causes pain to others with no other object than wanting to do so.

Arthur Schopenhauer
("On Ethics,"
in *Parerga and Paralipomena*)

The tendency of man's heart is towards evil from his youth.

Genesis 8:21

This early assessment of human nature from the Bible is frequently misinterpreted. It has no connection with the New Testament concept of original sin, in which man is born in a state of sin, irrespective of any actions he takes. What Genesis is suggesting is that evil and selfishness are more natural to man than goodness and altruism. Children are born selfish and have to be educated to generosity. As a friend of mine has pointed out: "When was the last time you heard a mother reproving her three-year-old son, 'Johnny, stop being so selfless and giving all your toys away to the other children'."

Although the Enlightenment contention that human beings are born good but corrupted by society is still popular today, it is easy to see the ways in which society humanizes people as they grow up. Ask parents whose children are retarded, or fat, or short, or ugly who taunts their children – adults or other children? Children, obviously.

So, evil must come from within human beings. Once, when I was attacked for asserting this, I answered: "If human beings are naturally good, then when their minds are free to wander their thoughts should be kind ones. And yet how many people would be pleased to have the fantasies that go through their mind before they fall asleep at night made known to the world? Most people, after all, don't fantasize about how to reduce world hunger."

The unnatural – that too is natural.
Johann Wolfgang von Goethe

More men become good through practice than by nature.
Democritus of Abdera

"Be yourself" is the worst advice you can give some people.
Tom Masson

Man is the only animal of which I am thoroughly and cravenly afraid. . . . There is less harm in a well-fed lion. It has no ideals, no sect, no party, no nation, no class: in short no reason for destroying anything it does not want to eat.
George Bernard Shaw
(Sixteen Self Sketches)

On the other hand . . .

I would tell a man who was drinking too much "Be a man," but I would not tell a crocodile who was eating too many explorers, "Be a crocodile."

G. K. Chesterton

Chesterton, a devout Catholic, and a contemporary of George Bernard Shaw's, disagreed with the playwright on most philosophical issues. Ironically, the above quote concerns appetites, the subject of the most famous personal encounter between them. When Chesterton, who was quite overweight, chanced upon the very thin Shaw on a London street, he declared, "Anyone who would see you, George, would think England was having a famine." Looking back at Chesterton's large frame, Shaw responded, "And anybody who would see you, Chesterton, would think you had caused it."

It disturbs me no more to find men base, unjust or selfish than to see apes mischievous, wolves savage, or the vulture ravenous for its prey.

Molière
(The Misanthrope)

For the world is hell, and men are on the one hand the tormented souls and on the other the devils in it.

Arthur Schopenhauer
("On the Suffering of the World")

God did not build Auschwitz and its crematoria. Men did....
The Holocaust may make faith in God difficult, but it makes faith
in man impossible.

**Dennis Prager and
Joseph Telushkin**
*(The Nine Questions
People Ask About Judaism)*

The human race has improved everything except the human race.
Adlai Stevenson
As the Democratic Party's
presidential candidate in 1952,
Stevenson elaborated on this theme:
"Nature is neutral. Man has wrested
from nature the power to make the
world a desert or to make the
deserts bloom. There is no evil in
the atom; only in men's souls."

I think... most men are trash.

Sigmund Freud

THE HUMAN CONDITION

Life

Life is like a game of cards. The hand that is dealt you represents determinism; the way you play it is free will.

Jawaharlal Nehru

Life can only be understood backwards, but it must be lived forwards.

Søren Kierkegaard

Life is the art of drawing sufficient conclusions from insufficient premises.

Samuel Butler
(Notebooks)

That life is worth living is the most necessary of assumptions and were it not assumed the most impossible of conclusions.

George Santayana
(The Life of Reason)

We're all in this together – by ourselves.

Lily Tomlin

The mass of men lead lives of quiet desperation.
Henry David Thoreau
(Walden)
And as my mother,
Helen Telushkin,
appends, "And recently,
they're not so quiet."

Nothing seems so tragic to one who is old as the death of one who is young, and this alone proves that life is a good thing.
Zoë Akins
(The Portrait of Tiero)

Meaning

He who has a why to live can bear with almost any how.
Friedrich Nietzsche

To have reason to get up in the morning, it is necessary to possess a guiding principle. A belief of some kind. A bumper sticker if you will.
Judith Guest
(Ordinary People)

A man is what he is, not what he used to be.
Yiddish proverb

In every age "the good old days" were a myth. No one ever thought they were good at the time. For every age has consisted of crises that seemed intolerable to the people who lived through them.

Brooks Atkinson
(Once Around the World)
Gustave Flaubert noted:
"Our ignorance of history causes
us to slander our own times."

The notion of primitive man possessing some inner peace which we civilized people have somehow lost, and need to regain, is a lot of nonsense. Your average New Guinean native lives not only in fear of his enemies, but in terror-struck dread of the unknown.
Gordon Linsley

On an ever larger scale "why not" is ceasing to be a question at all. It is becoming a kind of answer.

Prof. Earl Rovit
(quoted in Irving Kristol's
On the Democratic Idea in America)

If you think nobody cares if you're alive, try missing a couple of car payments.

Earl Wilson

INDIVIDUALITY AND INDIVIDUALS

Rabbi Zusha of Hanipol used to say, "If they ask me in the next world, 'Why were you not Moses?' I will know what to answer. But if they ask me, 'Why were you not Zusha?' I will have nothing to say."

Martin Buber
*(The Way of Man According
to the Teachings of Hasidism)*

If I try to be like him, who will be like me?

Yiddish proverb

It required only a moment to sever that head, but a century will not be sufficient to produce another like it.

Joseph LaGrange
(in 1794, on the guillotining of
French chemist Antoine Levoisier)

There is only one thing that can be said for Hitler's vicious life: it refutes the theory that only vast, impersonal forces, and not individuals, can shake the world.

George Will
(syndicated column,
November 4, 1976)

Don't compromise yourself. You are all you've got.

Janis Joplin.

One never cares for a crowd, only for a person. If I visualized a crowd I would never get started. The important thing is the individual.

Mother Teresa of Calcutta
(winner of the Nobel Peace Prize)
It has been said of her that "faced
with a mass of starving and dying
people, she does not see a crowd,
but simply a starving or dying person"
[George Gorree and Jean Barbier,
Love Without Boundaries].

Most people are other people. Their thoughts are someone else's opinions.

Oscar Wilde
(De Profundis)

Blaming The Institutions

The point is that it is always some institution that is at fault, never the individual. If garbage piles in the streets, that is not because people behave like pigs, but because the sanitation department is inefficient as, of course, it is. If Johnny doesn't learn, that is not because most children enjoy play more than work and a large minority have never been house-trained to check this propensity, but because the school system is deficient, as, of course, it is. If students smash up their college, that is not because all of us have a streak of hooliganism, which is not always easy to control, but because there is something very wrong with our higher educational system. If marriages break up, that proves that marriage is a bad institution. The same reasoning can be applied to murder, robbery, tax evasion, what you will.

Charles Issawi
(Issawi's Laws of Social Action)

LEARNING FROM MISTAKES AND EXPERIENCE

Mistakes

You are running very fast in the wrong direction.

Prof. Louis Ginzberg
(to an erring student at the
Jewish Theological Seminary)

If you are proved right you accomplish little; but if you are proved wrong, you gain much: you learn the truth.

Sefer Hasidim
(thirteenth-century
Jewish religious text)

A man who has committed a mistake and doesn't correct it, is committing a second mistake.

Confucius

There is something to be said for every error, but whatever may be said for it, the most important thing to be said about it is that it is erroneous.

G. K. Chesterton
(All is Grist)

We do not err because truth is difficult to see. It is visible at a glance. We err because it is more comfortable.

Alexander Solzhenitsyn

Experience

Everyone is perfectly willing to learn from unpleasant experience – if only the damage of the first lesson could be repaired.

George Lichtenberg

Never try to learn from an experience more than there is in it. There are some vivid and painful experiences that have little to teach us.

D. Sutten

We should be careful to get out of an experience only the wisdom that is in it – and stop there; lest we be like the cat that sits down on a hot stove lid. She will never sit down on a hot stove lid again – and that is well; but also she will never sit down on a cold one anymore.

Mark Twain
(Pudd'nhead Wilson's New Calendar)

Experience is a hard teacher because she gives the test first, the lesson afterwards.

Vernon Law

HAPPINESS AND PEACE OF MIND

It is not easy to find happiness in ourselves, and it is not possible to find it elsewhere.

Agnes Repplier

As if to confirm Agnes Repplier's comment, philosopher **Martin Buber** was fond of telling this Hasidic tale:

"**Rabbi Bunan** used to tell young men who came to him for the first time the story of Rabbi Eizik, son of Rabbi Yekel of Cracow. After many years of great poverty which had never shaken his faith in God, he dreamed someone bade him look for a treasure in Prague, under the bridge which leads to the king's palace. When the dream recurred a third time, Rabbi Eizik prepared for the journey and set out for Prague. But the bridge was guarded day and night and he did not dare to start digging. Nevertheless, he went to the bridge every morning, and kept walking around it till evening. Finally the captain of the guards, who had been watching him, asked in a kindly way whether he was looking for something or waiting for somebody. Rabbi Eizik told him of the dream which had brought him from a faraway country. The captain laughed: 'And so to please the dream, you, poor fellow, wore out your shoes to come here! As for having faith in dreams, if I had had it, I should have had to get going when a dream once told me to go to Cracow and dig for treasure under the stove in the room of a Jew – Eizik, son of Yekel, that was the name!' And he laughed again. Rabbi Eizik bowed, traveled home, [and] dug up the treasure.

"Take this story to heart. . . . There is something that can only be found in one place. It is a great treasure, which may be called the fulfillment of existence. The place where this treasure can be found is the place on which one stands."

Martin Buber
*(The Way of Man According
to the Teachings of Hasidism)*

The only people I know who are happy are people I don't know well.

Helen Telushkin

Before we set our hearts too much on anything, let us examine how happy are those who already possess it.

La Rochefoucald

You don't seem to realize that a poor person who is unhappy is in a better position than a rich person who is unhappy. Because the poor person has hope. He thinks money would help.

Jean Kerr

If we only wanted to be happy it would be easy; but we want to be happier than other people, which is almost always difficult, since we think them happier than they are.

Montesquieu

We have no more right to consume happiness without producing
it than to consume wealth without producing it.

George Bernard Shaw
(Candida)

If you haven't all the things you want, be grateful for the things
you don't have that you didn't want.

Unknown
(cited in John Gardner and
Francesca Gardner Reese's book
Know or Listen to Those Who Know)

Be happy while you're living
For you're a long time dead.

Scottish proverb

SUFFERING

Even the most innocent of men's affairs seem doomed to cause suffering. Pushing the lawnmower through tall wet grass, and enjoying the strong aroma of the morning, I found that the blades had cut a frog in half. I have not forgotten his eyes.

Christopher Morley
(Inward Ho)

Man has places in his heart which do not yet exist, and into them enters suffering, in order that they may have existence.

Léon Bloy
(quoted by Graham Greene
in the frontispiece of
The End of the Affair)

No rose without a thorn. But many a thorn without a rose.

Arthur Schopenhauer
(Essays and Aphorisms)

Each person suffers pain according to the condition of his soul and the level of his service to God. There is one who knows pain only because of his children, his parents, or his neighbors; another, of a higher state, suffers pain because of the whole city; but there is one of a very high state who suffers pain because of the troubles of the whole world.

Rabbi Nahman of Bratslav

In **George Bernard Shaw**'s *St. Joan*, there is an epilogue, set many years after the death of Joan of Arc, where the various characters who knew Joan speak to each other. A priest says that he is happy he saw the burning of Joan, because seeing its horror, he never could participate in such a thing again. Another character answers: "Must then a Christ perish in torment in every age to save those who have no imagination?"

OLD AGE

The girl who felt my stare and raised her eyes
Saw I was only an old man, and looked away
As people do when they see something not quite nice.

T. E. Matthews

One evil in old age is that, as your time is come, you think every little illness is the beginning of the end. When a man expects to be arrested, every knock at the door is an alarm.

Sydney Smith

The ultimate indignity is to be given a bedpan by a stranger who calls you by your first name.

Maggie Kahn
(quoted in Frank S. Pepper's
Handbook of Twentieth Century Quotations)

In twentieth-century America, the average life expectancy has risen from forty-seven to seventy-two years of age. However, together with this increased longevity, there is also a diminished respect for the elderly. This is not surprising. In traditional societies, elders were respected for their ties to the past, and for the wisdom they transmitted. In today's secular, scientific society, where knowledge is doubling every decade, the wisdom of the old is seen as out-of-date or out of touch. And now that the heroes of American society are generally actors, rock stars, and sports figures, it is no wonder that there is a poor regard for the physically decaying elderly. Yet this negativism towards old age –

underscored by the desperate need of so many Americans to look much younger than they are – is ultimately self-destructive. Since all of us expect to be old, it is surely in our own interest to cultivate respect for the future condition we all will share. Probably the reason we don't is because old age is seen the way death is: something we know happens to everyone, but that in our heart of hearts we don't believe will happen to us.

Ours seems to be the only nation on earth that asks its teen-agers what to do about world affairs, and tells its golden agers to go out and play.

Julian Grow

There are three ages of man: youth, middle age, and "you're looking terrific."

Francis Cardinal Spellman

I refuse to admit that I am more than fifty-two even if that does make my children illegitimate.

Lady Astor

In answer to young people who told him that he could not understand their problems, Fritz Kortner, the German actor, responded: "You were never as old as I am, on the other hand, I was as young as you are now."

Lore and Maurice Cowan
(The Wit of the Jews)

How old would you be if you didn't know how old you was?

Leroy Satchell Paige
(the oldest man ever to play
major league baseball)

Most people say that as you get old you have to give up things. I think you get old because you give up things.

Sen. Theodore Francis Green
(at age eighty-seven)
Green was a known political wit
in Washington. A Democrat, he
claimed that for years he had
wasted a great deal of money
giving taxi drivers large tips and
telling them to vote Democrat. He
eventually decided to give them
no tips at all, while instructing
them to vote Republican.

A man is only as old as the woman he feels.

Groucho Marx

The man who is too old to learn was probably always too old to learn.

Henry Haskins

DEATH

The Inevitability Of Death

To the men who told Socrates, "The Thirty Tyrants have condemned you to death," he replied, "And nature, them."

Montaigne

That the end of life should be death may sound sad; yet what other end can anything have?

George Santayana
*(Some Turns of Thought
in Modern Philosophy)*

Movie mogul Samuel Goldwyn once criticized **Dorothy Parker**: "Your stories are too sad, Dorothy. What the public wants are happy endings."

"Mr. Goldwyn," she responded. "Since the world was created, billions and billions of people have lived, and not a single one has had a happy ending."

I shall go to him, but he shall not return to me.

II Samuel 12:23
(David's lament on the
death of his infant son)

After the game the king and the pawn go into the same box.

Italian proverb

Wouldn't you think a man a prize fool if he burst into tears because he didn't live a thousand years ago? A man is as much a fool for shedding tears because he isn't going to be alive a thousand years from now.

Seneca
(Epistles)

While the above accept death's inevitability with grace, it is not hard to describe it with poetic morbidity. I find few images more disheartening than **Pascal**'s: "Let us imagine a number of men in chains, all condemned to death, where some are killed each day in the sight of the others, and those who remain see their own fate in that of their fellows, and wait their turn, looking at each other sorrowfully and without hope. It is an image of the condition of man" (*Pensées*).

In the nineteenth century **Turgenev** wrote, with similar light-heartedness: "Death is like a fisherman who catches fish in his net and leaves them for awhile in the water: the fish is still swimming but the net is around him, and the fisherman will draw him up – when he thinks fit" (*On the Eve*).

Death Comes As The End

Often I have wished myself dead, but well under my blanket, so that neither death nor man could hear me.

Georg Lichtenberg

Do not go gentle into that good night
Old age should burn and rave at close of day
Rage, rage, against the dying of the light.

Dylan Thomas
("Do not Go Gentle
Into that Good Night")

David Hume said to me, he was no more uneasy to think he should *not be* after this life than that he *had not been* before he began to exist.

James Boswell
(to Samuel Johnson)

Boswell saw that Hume's statement in no way helped calm Johnson's great fear of dying, and so he added: "Foote, Sir, told me that when he was very ill he was not afraid to die."

Johnson was not convinced. "It is not true, Sir. Hold a pistol to Foote's or to Hume's breast and threaten to kill them and you'll see how they behave."

Whoever has lived long enough to find out what life is, knows how deep a debt of gratitude we owe to Adam, the first great benefactor of our race. He brought death into the world.

Mark Twain
(Pudd'nhead Wilson's Calendar)

Strangely enough, Mark Twain, who brought joy to millions of people, was extraordinarily attracted to death. After the death of his daughter Jean, this great comedic talent wrote what has to be one of the most melancholy passages ever written: "Would I bring her back to life if I could do it? I would not. If a word would do it, I would beg for strength to withhold the word. And I would have the strength; I am sure of it. In her loss I am almost bankrupt, and my life is bitterness, but I am content; for she has been enriched with the most precious of all gifts. . . death. I have never wanted any released friend of mine restored to life since I reached manhood. I felt this way when Susy passed away, and later my wife, and later Mr. Rogers. When Clara met me at the station and told me Mr. Rogers had died suddenly that morning, my thought was: 'Oh, favorite of fortune – fortunate all his long and lovely life – fortunate to his latest moment!' The reporters said there were tears of sorrow in my eyes. True – but they were for *me*, not for him. He had suffered no loss. All the fortunes he had ever made before were poverty compared with this one" ("The Death of Jean," *Harper's Bazaar*, 1911).

Life does not cease to be funny when people die any more than it ceases to be serious when people laugh.

George Bernard Shaw

One man wants to live but can't, another man can – but doesn't want to.

Yiddish proverb

Immortality

Millions long for immortality who do not know what to do with themselves on a rainy Sunday afternoon.

Susan Ertz

The fact of having been born is a bad augury for immortality.
George Santayana
(The Life of Reason)

The universe is a stairway leading nowhere unless man is immortal.
E. Y. Mullins

The ancients dreaded death; the Christian can only fear dying.
J. C. and A. W. Hare
(Success at Truth)

For both Christians and Jews the major issue in faith is generally the existence of God, and not whether or not there is an afterlife. For once one believes that there is a good and all-powerful God, it follows that there must be a life beyond this one. The only possible explanation for God allowing so much suffering and injustice is that there is another dimension of existence where there is redress. Strangely enough, there is no clear reference to afterlife in the Torah. Perhaps this is because the opening books of the Bible were written in the aftermath of Hebrew slavery in Egypt. The Egyptian experience had taught the children of Israel how dangerous an obsession with afterlife could become. Consider that the major achievement of many of the Pharaohs was an enormous tomb for themselves, and in the process of erecting it, thousands of slaves were worked to death. The holiest book of the Egyptians, *The Book of the Dead,* reflects their obsession with afterlife. Perhaps the Bible did not raise the issue of afterlife because it recognized that when it becomes a central issue in religion, it diverts people's attention from their responsibilities in *this* world.

One short sleep past we wake eternally
And death shall be no more; death thou shalt die.

John Donne
("Death Be Not Proud")

If we had the offer of immortality here below, who would accept this sorrowful gift?

Jean Jacques Rousseau
(Emile)

I don't want to achieve immortality through my work. I want to achieve it through not dying.

Woody Allen

Last Words, Almost Last Words, And Epitaphs

A poor man in search of a lost bag of pennies, passed through a city where he found fame and fortune. Do you suppose he would resume his search for the missing pennies?

Count Valentine Potocki
(before his execution, 1749)
Potocki, a Polish nobleman, was
sentenced to death for converting to
Judaism, a capital crime in eighteenth-
century Poland. He was offered
clemency if he returned to Christianity.
The above was his response.

Now it is time to go – I to die and you to live; which is the better is not known to anyone but God.

Socrates
(in Plato's *Apology*)

I have fought a good fight. I have finished my course. I have kept the faith.

Paul of Tarsus
(II Timothy, 4:17)

Be of good comfort, Master Ridley, and play the man: we shall this day light such a candle, by God's grace, in England, as I trust shall never be put out.

Hugh Latimer
(Bishop of Worcester and
Protestant martyr burned with
Nicholas Ridley on charges of
heresy, Oxford, 1555)

Even in the valley of the shadow of death two and two do not make six.

Leo Tolstoy
(when, as he was dying,
he was urged to return to
the Russian Orthodox Church)

It is not surprising that some of the most eloquent final words come from prominent religious or philosophical martyrs (Socrates, St. Paul, Hugh Latimer), or from great writers such as Tolstoy.

But to my mind, none of their words exceed in power the last known words of **Isaac Rosenzweig,** a poultry farmer in Slovakia, Poland, who was murdered by the Nazis during World War II. Crowded with hundreds of other Jews into a cattle car bound for Auschwitz, and surrounded by hostile and jeering Polish neighbors, Rosenzweig turned to them: "Please, go to my house and give water and food to the poultry. They have had nothing to eat or drink all day." **Eliezer Berkovits,** who recounts this incident in his book *Faith After the Holocaust,* concludes: "Because of what man did to Isaac Rosenzweig I have no faith in man; because of Isaac, in spite of it all, I have faith in the future of man."

Now he is a legend when he would have preferred to be a man.
Jacqueline Kennedy

I would have written of me on my stone: I had a lover's quarrel with the world.

Robert Frost

He did his best – and it wasn't good enough.

Arthur Koestler's
epitaph for himself.
Koestler committed
suicide with his wife.

If there's another world, he lives in bliss
If there is none, he made the best of this.

Robert Burns
(epitaph on William Muir)

Die, my dear doctor? That's the last thing I shall do.

Viscount Henry Palmerston
(English statesman who died in 1865)

At last she sleeps alone.

Robert Benchley's
suggested epitaph for a
promiscuous female acquaintance.

They couldn't hit an elephant at this dist. . . .

Gen. John Sedgwick
(1864)
Sedgwick was incautiously
looking over the parapet at the
Civil War battle of Spotsylvania when
he gave his troops this assurance.

If I had any epitaph. . . it would be to say that I had disturbed the
sleep of my generation.

Adlai Stevenson

Prophetic. . .

My last words to you, my son and successor, are never trust
the Russians.

Abdur Rahman Khan
(Emir of Afghanistan
who died in 1901)

And Unprophetic...

There will be no proof that I was ever a writer.

Franz Kafka
Just before he died in 1924, the
Austrian novelist asked his friend
Max Brod to burn all his writings.
Brod promised, but subsequently
could not bring himself to do it.

SUICIDE

A suicide is a sentinel who has deserted his post.

Bahya ibn Pakuda
(medieval Jewish philosopher,
in *Duties of the Heart*)

There is only one philosophical problem that is really serious, and that is suicide. To decide whether life is worth living or not is to answer the fundamental question in philosophy.

Albert Camus
(The Myth of Sisyphus)

God has reserved to himself the right to determine the end of life, because He alone knows the goal to which it is His will to lead it. It is for Him alone to justify a life or to cast it away.

Dietrich Bonhoeffer
(Lutheran minister
executed by the Nazis)

Suicide is not abominable because God forbids it. God forbids it because it is abominable.

Immanuel Kant
(Lecture at Königsberg)

In both Judaism and Christianity suicide is defined as self-inflicted *murder*. Jewish law rules that suicides are to be buried at the side of the cemetery and denied the normal mourning rites. But these rulings were apparently enacted mainly to discourage would-be suicides. In practice, rabbis almost never defined a self-inflicted killing as suicide (usually pronouncing it as accidental or due to momentary insanity), because they recognized that imposing the law would punish only the family, not the suicide. In Catholicism suicide is the ultimate sin for a believer, because it despairs of God.

Some religious thinkers have tried to prove *logically* that suicide is worse than murder. Thus the medieval Jewish philosopher Bahya, cited above, wrote, "The nearer the relation to the murdered person, the more heinous the crime...and man is closest to himself." St. Augustine said, "Parricide is more wicked than homicide, but suicide is the most wicked of all" (*On Patience*). Catholic theologian G. K. Chesterton reached an even more extreme conclusion: "The man who kills a man, kills a man. The man who kills himself, kills all men; as far as he is concerned he wipes out the world" (*On Orthodoxy*). But, it is on the grounds of logic that most people reject this argument that suicide is more evil than murder because in the case of suicide the person who is dead wanted to be dead, whereas in the case of murder the person who is dead wanted to be alive.

There is far less opposition to suicide among most secular thinkers. Marya Mannes expressed a characteristic secularist view: "The right to choose death when life no longer holds meaning is not only the next liberation but the last human right" (*Last Rights*). And statistical studies confirm much higher rates of suicide among nonbelievers.

The thought of suicide is a great consolation; with the help of it one gets through many a bad night.

Friedrich Nietzsche

Suicide is about life, being in fact the sincerest form of criticism life gets.

Wilfred Sheed
(The Good Word)

There are many who dare not kill themselves for fear of what the neighbors would say.

Cyril Connolly
(The Unquiet Grave)

Your health comes first – you can always hang yourself later.
Yiddish proverb

WHO IS RICH?

Who is rich? One who is happy with what he has.

Talmud
(Pirkei Avot, 4:1)

Man never has what he wants because what he wants is everything.

C. F. Ramuz
(What is Man?)

Many men hoard for the future husbands of their wives.

Solomon Ibn Gabirol
(medieval Jewish philosopher,
in *Pearls of Wisdom*)

Told that a certain man had acquired great wealth, a sage asked: "Has he also acquired the days in which to spend it?"

Solomon Ibn Gabirol
(Pearls of Wisdom)

For what shall it profit a man, if he shall gain the whole world and lose his own soul?

Mark: 8:36

If you want to know how rich you really are, find out what would be left of you tomorrow if you should lose every dollar you own tonight.

William H. H. Boetcker

Scott Fitzgerald: "The rich are different from us."
Ernest Hemingway: "Yes, they have more money."
Peter De Vries: "The rich aren't like us, they pay less taxes."

To suppose as we all suppose, that we could be rich and not behave as the rich behave, is like supposing that we could drink all day and stay sober.

Logan Pearsall Smith

There are a handful of people whom money won't spoil, and we count ourselves among them.

Mignon McLaughlin

BETWEEN MAN AND
THE WORLD

DEMOCRACY IS THE WORST FORM OF GOVERNMENT, EXCEPT...

Democracy is the worst form of government that man has ever devised, except for all those other forms that have been tried from time to time.

Winston Churchill

Freedom is the freedom to say that two plus two equals four. If that is granted, all else follows.

George Orwell
(Nineteen Eighty-Four)

If a nation values anything more than freedom, it will lose its freedom; and the irony of it is that if it is comfort or money that it values more, it will lose that too.

W. Somerset Maugham

Democracy [has] at least one merit, namely that a Member of Parliament cannot be stupider than his constituents, for the more stupid he is, the more stupid they were to elect him.

Bertrand Russell

Man's capacity for justice makes democracy possible, but man's inclination to injustice makes democracy necessary.

Reinhold Niebuhr

As I would not be a *slave*, so I would not be a *master*. This expresses my idea of democracy. Whatever differs from this, to the extent of the difference, is no democracy.

Abraham Lincoln
(August 1, 1858)

Democracy gives every man the right to be his own oppressor.

James Russell Lowell
(The Bigelow Papers)

What's Wrong With Democracy?

I should be very sorry to find myself on board a ship in which the voices of the cook and loblolly boys counted for as much as those of the officers, upon a question of steering, or reefing topsails, or where the "great heart" of the crew was called upon to settle the ship's course.

T. H. Huxley
(On the Natural Inequality of Man)

Huxley's statement is the rationale of all dictators. It is effective, but also demagogic. He assumes that the running of a government, and the moral decisions it entails, are scientific skills like "steering or reefing topsails," the knowledge of which is restricted to the few. Defenders of democracy concede the unreliability of the "great heart" as a navigating device. But, as **Calvin Coolidge** put it: "It would be folly to argue that people cannot and will not make grave mistakes. They know it, they pay the penalty, but compared with the mistakes which have been made by every kind of autocracy, they are unimportant."

The weakness of democracy – the reason why Karl Marx and others must be laughing in their graves – is precisely that it's about winning votes. No government can afford to have a survival strategy because that means losing votes.

Andrew Knight
(Newsweek,
January 13, 1975)

The reason democracy doesn't work is that, while bribing of individual votes is illegal, the bribery of whole classes of voters is not.

from the **Dublin Opinion**
(cited in *Quote* magazine,
October 29, 1967)

POLITICS

Political Ethics

In politics it is necessary either to betray one's country or the electorate. I prefer to betray the electorate.

Charles de Gaulle
(justifying his Algerian policy)

Betraying the electorate by making irresponsible and undeliverable promises is a characteristic feature of twentieth-century American presidential campaigns. Nonetheless, one cannot altogether blame the candidates for this. For example, the United States has never fought in a more justifiable war than World War II. Yet Franklin Delano Roosevelt apparently believed that the public would vote him out of office if he argued for America joining the war against Hitler. And so he won the 1940 election with the promise: "And while I am talking to you, mothers and fathers, I give you one more assurance. I have said this before but I shall say it again and again. Your boys are not going to be sent into any foreign war" (October 30, 1940).

Twenty-four years later, Lyndon Johnson soundly defeated Sen. Barry Goldwater, arguing that the Republican candidate would drag America into war in Vietnam. Instead, Johnson *promised,* "We are not going to send American boys nine or ten thousand miles away from home to do what Asian boys ought to be doing for themselves" (October 21, 1964). A week before the election he stated, "There can and will be, as long as I am President, peace for all Americans" (October 17, 1964). Johnson won a resounding victory and proceeded to send half a million troops into Vietnam.

Who is at fault for such things? The *politicians* who make promises they cannot or will not keep, or the *electorate* which makes clear to pollsters and candidates that it will vote against anyone who tells them the painful truth and the painful price that will have to be paid?

One thing is certain: forcing our candidates to make lofty, impossible promises of permanent peace, runs the risk of turning us, in **Irving Kristol**'s words, into either "the most high-minded people who ever lived or the most hypocritical" (*On the Democratic Idea in America*).

There is an increased demand for codes of ethics in politics, although most officeholders are sworn in with their hand resting on one.

Bill Vaughn

The tragedy of politics: "If you live with pirates, you must behave like a pirate" (Bismarck); but if you behave like a pirate you end by becoming one yourself.

Charles Issawi
(Issawi's Laws of Social Action)

I would rather fail in a cause that someday will triumph than win in a cause that I know someday will fail.

Woodrow Wilson

Wilson's moral self-assurance reminds me of Henry Clay's 1850 statement: "I would rather be right than be President." Years later, when a Congressman Springer used Clay's words in reference to himself, Speaker of the House **Thomas Reed** responded: "The gentleman need not worry. He will never be either."

He proved that a man could be both decent and political.
Sen. Hubert H. Humphrey
(eulogizing Adlai Stevenson in 1965)

Political Campaigns

The hardest thing about any political campaign is how to win without proving that you are unworthy of winning.
Adlai Stevenson

If the Republicans stop telling lies about us, we will stop telling the truth about them.
Adlai Stevenson
(1952)
Ironically, this quip had been used fifty years earlier by the Republican senator from New York, Chauncey Depew, and directed against the Democrats.

Stevenson's wit survived even the loss of an election. After his defeat by Eisenhower in 1952, he was asked how he felt. "I am reminded of a story that a fellow townsman of ours used to tell – **Abraham Lincoln.** They asked him how he felt once after an unsuccessful election. He said that he felt like a little boy who had stubbed his toe in the dark. He said that he was too old to cry, but that it hurt too much to laugh."

There isn't any great public outcry for me to do this. I just want the office.

Lt. Gov. James Blair of Missouri,
declaring his candidacy
for a second term.

Vote for the man who promises least; he'll be the least disappointing.
Bernard Baruch

Baruch's advice exemplifies the general cynicism Americans have for politicians. Similarly, humorist **Kim Hubbard** stated: "We'd all like to vote for the best man, but he's never a candidate."

Have you ever seen a candidate talking to a rich person on television?
Art Buchwald

Political Heckling And Invective

During a campaign speech, Republican **Theodore Roosevelt** was constantly interrupted by a heckler. Roosevelt finally asked the man why he so vigorously opposed him.

"Because I am a Democrat," the heckler said.

"Why are you a Democrat?" Roosevelt asked.

"Because my father was a Democrat and my grandfather was a Democrat."

"And suppose your father and grandfather had been jackasses, what would you be then?"

"A Republican," the heckler responded.

When Gov. **Al Smith** of New York was campaigning, a heckler kept on bothering him. Finally, the heckler shouted, "Tell them all you know, Al. It won't take long." Smith responded, "I'll tell them all we both know and it won't take any longer."

I have noted with interest your suggestion as to where those who vote for my opponent should go. While I understand and sympathize with your deep motivation I think that our side should try to refrain from raising the religious issue.

> **John F. Kennedy**
> (the first successful Catholic candidate
> for President, October 19, 1960,
> in a telegram to Harry Truman)
> Truman had told a San Antonio
> audience that anyone who votes
> for Nixon "should go to hell."

Political Ideologies And Parties

There is no Republican way or Democratic way to clean the streets.

> **Fiorello H. La Guardia**
> (mayor of New York City)

There are many men of principle in both parties in America, but there is no party of principle.

> **Alexis de Tocqueville**

The trouble with the Republican Party is that it has not had a new idea for thirty years. I am not speaking as a politician. I am speaking as an historian.

Woodrow Wilson

The middle of the road . . . is the worst place to drive.

Robert Frost,
reacting to constant description
of the Eisenhower administration
as "middle-of-the-road".

A liberal is a man too broad-minded to take his own side in a quarrel.

Robert Frost

A man becomes conservative at that moment in his life when he suddenly realizes he has something to conserve.

Eric Julber

The Presidency

When we got into office, the thing that surprised me most was to find that things were just as bad as we'd been saying they were.

John F. Kennedy

Presidents quickly realize that while a single act might destroy the world they live in, no one single decision can make life suddenly better or can turn history around for the good.

Lyndon B. Johnson

A president's hardest task is not to do what is right, but to know what is right.

Lyndon B. Johnson

When I was a boy, I was told that anyone could become President; now I'm beginning to believe it.

Clarence Darrow

The Vice Presidency

I am nothing but tomorrow I may be everything.

John Adams
(The First Vice President)

Take it to the vice president – he needs something to keep him awake.

Theodore Roosevelt,
to a White House butler who was
uncertain where to place a chandelier
that Roosevelt had ordered.

Once there were two brothers. One ran away to sea, and the other was elected vice president, and nothing was ever heard of either of them again.

Thomas Marshall
(American vice president,
1913-21; in his book
Recollections)

Final Thoughts

Sheridan's parliamentary colleagues had brought in an extremely unpopular message, on which they were defeated. He then said that he had often heard of people knocking out their brains against a wall, but never before had known of anyone building a wall expressly for that purpose.

**John Gardner and
Francesca Gardner Reese**
(Know or Listen to Those Who Know)

There is just one rule for politicians all over the world. Don't say in power what you say in opposition: if you do, you have only to carry out what the other fellows have found impossible.

John Galsworthy
(Maid in Waiting)

Too bad that all the people who know how to run the country are busy driving taxicabs and cutting hair.

George Burns

INTELLECTUALS

It is no defense whatever for an intellectual to say that he was duped, since that is what, as an intellectual, he should never allow to happen to him.

Granville Hicks
(Where We Came Out)

Hicks was referring here to the well-known propensity of certain intellectuals to support oppressive regimes, and then to claim they were misled. For instance, American playwright Lillian Hellman supported Stalin's infamous purge trials, attacked those who organized relief for Finnish victims of Soviet aggression, and continued supporting Russia even after the Hitler-Stalin pact. Confronted with irrefutable evidence of Stalin's murder of over 18 million people during the very years she had supported him, Hellman conceded she had been misled, and then proceeded to label the people who had called her a pro-Communist as "scoundrels."

Even those intellectuals who denounce totalitarian regimes often find it difficult to admit their personal responsibility for having previously supported them. In recanting her support of Communist regimes, Susan Sontag declared: "When I was in Cuba and North Vietnam, it was not clear to me that they would become Soviet satellites, but history has been very cruel" (Michiko Kakutani, "For Susan Sontag, the Illusions of the 60's Have Been Dissipated," *New York Times*, November 11, 1980). Since it was clear to virtually everyone else that both these countries were Soviet satellites, Sontag's statement is, by and large, disingenuous and merely an avoidance of self-criticism. She supported Communist regimes, and then blamed history for her own error.

Jonathan Mirsky has written with rare candor of the readiness of many leftist intellectuals to be duped. When he visited China in 1972, he came back with glowing, uncritical reports. Seven years later he admitted that "throughout our trip. . . we sheathed the critical faculties, which had been directed at our own Government, and. . . humbly helped to insert the rings in our own noses." As one of Mirsky's former guides told him when they met again in 1979, "*We* wanted to deceive you. But *you* wanted to be deceived."

I would rather be governed by the first 300 names in the Boston telephone book than by the faculty of Harvard University.

William F. Buckley, Jr.

The job of intellectuals is to come up with ideas, and all we've been producing is footnotes.

Theodore H. White
One of my professors at Columbia
University, **Arthur Hertzberg,** used
to say that "most dissertations are four
thousand footnotes in search of a thesis."

The trouble with the world is that the stupid are cocksure and the intelligent are full of doubt.

Bertrand Russell
(Autobiography)

Those who truly believe in the doctrine of infallibility, like the popes, pray to God for guidance before they make decisions. Those who do not, like professors, do not pray to God because they think they have no need to.

Prof. Sigmund Diamond
(cited in Charles Issawi's
Issawi's Laws of Social Action)

If everybody contemplates the infinite instead of fixing the drains, many of us will die of cholera.

John Rich

A professor's opinion: not Shakespeare is the thing, but the commentaries on him.

Anton Chekhov

Miscellaneous

What reason is there to think that anyone was ever corrupted by a book? This. . . question, oddly enough, is asked. . . by people – e.g. university professors and schoolteachers – whose very lives provide all the answers one could want. After all, if you believe that no one was ever corrupted by a book, you have also to believe that no one was ever improved by a book (or a play or a movie). You have to believe, in other words, that. . . all education is morally trivial. No one, not even a university professor, really believes that.

Irving Kristol
(On the Democratic Idea in America)

There are two very bad things in this American land of ours, the worship of money and the worship of intellect. Both money and intellect are regarded as good in themselves, and you consequently see the possessor of either eager to display his possessions to the public, and win public recognition of the fact. But intellect is as essentially *subordinate* a good as money is. It is good only as a minister and purveyor to right affections.

Henry James

He was in the class of intellectuals who want their indifference to public notice to be universally recognized.

Tom Stoppard
(about James Joyce, whom
Stoppard lambasted in his
musical *Travesties*)

Not many intellectuals have the courage to admit they pick up a book and look first for their name in the index.

Irving Howe
(*New York Times* interview,
January 1, 1969)

These quotes of intellectuals about themselves are disproportionately negative, I realize, but then this disproportion itself points up a great virtue of intellectuals: their greater willingness than the general public to be introspective and self-critical.

WAR

It is well that war is so terrible or we would grow too fond of it.

Gen. Robert E. Lee
(at the Battle of Fredericksburg)

The question we should ask about war is not whether it is evil, but why, if it so universally condemned as evil, are so many wars fought? Why do human beings *say* they hate war when their actions show they are also strongly attracted to it? In his book *Prejudices,* social theorist **Robert Nisbet** delineates very precisely what it is that makes war attractive. It releases people from their normally mundane, repetitious and boring lives. Nisbet recalls that when he was first appointed to a university post he thought he had achieved the good life. But shortly thereafter, the United States entered World War II and his formerly exciting job suddenly seemed irrelevant and boring. So, despite a draft deferment, he enlisted. During the war, he experienced both horror and fear but also the greatest exhilaration he had ever felt. And he found the same to be true of most other soldiers.

Man lives by habits indeed, but what he lives for is thrills and excitements. . . . From time immemorial war has been. . . the supremely thrilling excitement.

William James
(*Memories and Studies*)

War. . . can be exciting and even enjoyable – however disgusting in retrospect. I can honestly say that I relished nearly every minute of it: and that when at last I was wounded and had to leave the field, I felt a sense of bitter deprivation.... [My experience in war] enabled me to understand what I should not have understood before, why war, with all its horrors and injustices and its danger to all that civilization stands for, has yet persisted so long.

Lord Robbins
(Autobiography of an Economist)

War also satisfies the need for community, especially the kind of close community created under emergency conditions. Many veterans have told me that their army friendships were the most intense friendships they had ever had, and often forged within days. It is not surprising that civilian friendships with fellow workers, or neighbors, or tennis partners seem less vital.

Get in a tight spot in combat, and some guy will risk his ass to help you. Get in a tight spot in peacetime, and you go it all alone.

Brendan Francis

Look at the Swiss! They have enjoyed peace for centuries and what have they produced? The cuckoo clock.

Graham Greene and Orson Welles
(The Third Man)

War, Robert Nisbet notes, is responsible for a great deal of technological and social progress. Much of what is developed for wartime use subsequently raises the quality of life in peacetime. Commercial radio and air travel developed as by-products of the technological development that occurred during World War I. Many of the most important medical advances were made during wartime: new surgical techniques, new drugs and new procedures in anesthesia. Historically, many of the major advances in engineering have been the result of wars. Nor is this surprising. Clearly, war activates technological creativity in a way that peace seldom does.

The socioeconomic consequences of war are as profound as the technological ones. The American Depression came to an end only when the United States entered World War II. Before Pearl Harbor, the U.S. still suffered intolerably high unemployment, but once the war began the country started on a steadily upward economic spiral. Nisbet points out that "economics has not yet learned the secrets of depression and prosperity but war has."

Wars have also democratized societies. In wartime, merit is more vital than heredity, and so officers are drawn from the ranks, and not just from the upper classes. Granting women the right to vote, which was constitutionally affirmed in the United States in 1920, was largely a result of the active role of women in the work force during World War I. The black movement for equal rights was significantly accelerated by black involvement in World War II.

Obviously, this is not the whole picture. Most of the technological advances generated by war are devices to kill. War has caused the physical and psychological destruction of millions of people. But knowing all this is clearly an insufficient impetus to stop wars. If indeed that is our goal (as our warhating rhetoric suggests), we will have to find other ways to relieve boredom, create unified communities, and stimulate creativity than fighting a common enemy. In other words, we will have to actually improve human nature.

War: Its Horrors And Absurdities

The best way to convince a man that war is not an exciting adventure is to kill half his friends, drop a bomb on his family's home, and relieve him of a limb or two.

Nick Downe
(British television
war cameraman)
Downe continued:
"A less dramatic but quite
effective form of education
is to show events like these
on color television."

In peace, sons bury their fathers; in war, fathers bury their sons.
Herodotus

It became necessary to destroy the town to save it.
Unknown U.S. Army Major
Perhaps the most infamous
quote to come out of the Vietnam
War, this was the explanation
offered an Associated Press
reporter for the destruction of
the Vietnamese town of Ben Tre.

How good bad music and bad reasons sound when we march against an enemy.
Friedrich Nietzsche

To save your world you asked this man to die:
Would this man, could he see you now, ask why?

W. H. Auden
("Epitaph for an Unknown Soldier")

You can't say civilization don't advance...for in every war they
kill you in a new way.

Will Rogers
(The Autobiography of Will Rogers)

They came three thousand miles and died
To keep the past upon its throne.

Epitaph
over the tomb of two British
soldiers who died in a skirmish
at Concord Bridge, 1775.

This year you're a hero. Next year you'll be a disabled veteran.
And after that you'll be a cripple.

Unnamed doctor
(to the World War II wounded
at an army rehabilitation center)

It takes twenty years or more of peace to make a man; it takes
only twenty seconds of war to kill him.

Baudouin I of Belgium
(in an address to joint
session of Congress,
May 12, 1959)

I believe in compulsory cannibalism. If people were forced to eat what they killed there would be no more war.

Abbie Hoffman
(Revolution for the Hell of It)

Field Marshall Haig. . . drowned hundreds of men in the mud-holes of Flanders [in World War I]. Lloyd George was obliged to sanction this because Haig was such an important and respected leader. Such people simply have to be allowed to do their stuff. How paradoxical it is that a man who uses heroin may get a twenty-year sentence for what he does to himself.

Saul Bellow
(Herzog)

Renunciation of chemical and biological warfare, and humane treatment for prisoners of war. . . are certainly marks of civilized peoples, but on a more fundamental level such matters are little different from a convention requiring cannibals to eat with knives and forks. "Civilized warfare" is inherently a self-contradiction.

Rabbi J. David Bleich
(Contemporary Halakhic Problems)

Can anything be more ridiculous than that a man has a right to kill me because he lives on the other side of the water, and because his ruler has a quarrel with mine, although I have none with him?

Blaise Pascal
(Pensées)

Final Thoughts

A prisoner of war is a man who tries to kill you and fails, and then asks you not to kill him.

Winston Churchill

He is known as Alexander the Great because he killed more people of more different kinds than any other man of his time. He did this in order to impress Greek culture upon them.

Will Cuppy
*(The Decline and Fall of
Practically Everybody)*

In a war of ideas it is people who get killed.

Stanislaw Lec

Human beings do not fight for economic systems: who would be willing to die for capitalism? Certainly not the capitalists.

Sidney Hook
(Philosophy and Public Policy)

The Marxist belief that wars are motivated by economic considerations is generally false. Rather it is *ideas* that cause most wars. Was Hitler primarily motivated by economics? Are the Arab states in their wars against Israel? Was the American Civil War primarily a result of economic conflict? Was it economics that prompted Ho Chi Minh to invade South Vietnam?

The one thing I cannot forgive the Arabs for is that they forced our sons to kill their sons.

Golda Meir
(late Prime Minister of Israel)

In the late 1960s, when Israel was fighting a slow and deadly war of attrition with Egypt, **Golda Meir** was asked when there would be peace with Egypt. "I have given instructions," she answered, "that I be informed every time one of our soldiers is killed, even if it is the middle of the night. When President Nasser leaves instructions that he be awakened in the middle of the night if an Egyptian soldier is killed, there will be peace."

Beasts do not fight collectively. Who has ever seen ten lions fight ten bulls? Yet how often do 20,000 armed Christians fight 20,000 armed Christians?

Erasmus
(Complaint of Peace)

What scoundrels we would be if we did for ourselves what we stand ready to do for Italy?

Conte Camillo Benso di Cavour

If World War III is fought with atom bombs the war after that will be fought with stones.

Albert Einstein
(attributed)

PACIFISM AND ITS OPPONENTS

Offer the wicked man no resistance. On the contrary, if anyone hits you on the right cheek, offer him the other as well.

Jesus
(Matthew 5:38-39)

Possibly the three most important modern views on pacifism have been expressed by Mahatma Gandhi, Bertrand Russell, and Sidney Hook. Their positions state all the major arguments for and against turning the other cheek.

I would like you [the British] to lay down the arms you have as being useless for saving you or humanity. You will invite Herr Hitler and Signor Mussolini to take what they want of the countries you call your possessions. . . . If these gentlemen choose to occupy your homes you will vacate them. If they do not give you free passage out, you will allow yourselves, man, woman and child to be slaughtered, but you will refuse to owe allegiance to them.

Mahatma Gandhi
(Non-Violence in Peace and War)

I am as certain as I am dictating these lines that the stoniest German heart will melt [if only the Jews] . . . adopt active non-violence. Human nature. . . unfailingly responds to the advances of love. I do not despair of his [Hitler's] responding to human suffering even though caused by him.

Mahatma Gandhi
(in his newspaper *Harijan*,
December 17 and 24, 1938
and January 7, 1939)

Gandhi: "Hitler killed five million Jews. It is the greatest crime of our time. But the Jews should have offered themselves to the butcher's knife. They should have thrown themselves into the sea from cliffs."

Louis Fischer: "You mean that the Jews should have committed collective suicide?"

Gandhi: "Yes, that would have been heroism."

(June, 1946; quoted in
Gideon Shimoni's *Gandhi,
Satyagraha and the Jews*)

We did not proclaim as did Jesus, the son of our people, and as you do, the teaching of nonviolence, because we believe that a man must sometimes use force to save himself or even more his children.

Martin Buber
(responding to Gandhi's advice
of 1938–39 about how Jews
should respond to Hitler)

While Gandhi's support of pacifism was generally rooted in his belief that it is always better to be killed than to kill, in the statement that follows his pacifism is based on the idea that life itself is the highest value, a position associated with Bertrand Russell, and popularly espoused today in the West.

What difference does it make to the dead, the orphans, and the homeless, whether the mad destruction is wrought under the name of totalitarianism or the holy name of liberty or democracy?

Mahatma Gandhi

I am for controlled nuclear disarmament, but, if the Communists cannot be induced to agree to it, then I am for unilateral disarmament, even if it means the horrors of Communist domination.

Bertrand Russell

Sidney Hook, a passionate opponent of pacifist ideology, disagrees. He notes that "the foolishness of such a position is apparent, since it can only harden Communist intransigence."

It is better to be a live jackal than a dead lion – for jackals, not men.

Sidney Hook
(Philosophy and Public Policy)
Hook goes on to note that: "Men
who have the moral courage to fight
for freedom intelligently, and,
if necessary to die for it, have
the best prospects of avoiding the
fate of both live jackals and dead
lions. Survival is not the be-all and
end-all of a life worthy of man."

Sometimes the worst thing we can know about a man is that he has survived. Those who say that life is worth living at any cost have already written for themselves an epitaph of infamy, for there is no cause and no person they will not betray to stay alive.

Sidney Hook
(Philosophy and Public Policy)

Heretofore, all moral codes held that at times life must be sacrificed for the sake of morality. Pacifism holds the direct opposite: morality must be sacrificed for the sake of life.

Dennis Prager

Pacifism means biology takes precedence over morality: long lives are more valuable than good lives.

Dennis Prager

Final Thoughts

When British prime minister Neville Chamberlain gave in to Hitler's demands at Munich in 1938, thereby acceding to the Nazi take-over of Czechoslovakia, **Winston Churchill** warned: "You were given the choice between war and dishonor. You chose dishonor, and you will have war."

Sometime they'll give a war and nobody will come.

Carl Sandburg
(The People, Yes)

There is hardly such a thing as a war in which it makes no difference who wins. Nearly always one side stands more or less for progress, the other side more or less for reaction.

George Orwell

I have always been against the pacifists during the war, and against the jingoists at the end.

Winston Churchill

THE TOTALITARIAN TEMPTATION

You ask if parties other than the Bolsheviks will be allowed to exist? Emphatically! They will exist in prison.

Vladimir Ilich Lenin

It is not my business to do justice. It is my business to annihilate and exterminate – that's all.

Hermann Goering
(on the fate of those
who opposed Nazism)

Tolstoy was once asked if he didn't see the difference between reactionary and revolutionary repression. He replied that there was, of course, a difference: "the difference between cat shit and dog shit."

Arnold Beichman
(Nine Lies About America)

It is common in the West to see Nazism and Communism as opposites, with Nazism supposedly representing the radical right and Communism the radical left. However, since totalitarianism unites the two, they are actually more similar than dissimilar – a fact that their leaders, at least, have always understood. Hitler declared: "There is more that binds us to Bolshevism than separates us from it. . . . I have always made allowances for this circumstance, and given orders that former Communists are to be admitted to the Party at once. . . . The Social-Democrat and the trade-union boss will never make a National-Socialist, but the Communist always will" (quoted in Herman Rauschning's *Hitler Speaks*).

In the early 1930s, Nazis and Communists cooperated in strikes in Germany designed to bring down the democratic Weimar government, and German Communist leader Karl Radek predicted that the Nazi Brownshirts would be a reserve of future Communist recruits. Stalin's secret police exchanged information with Hitler's secret police on potential enemies, and in 1939, Hitler and Stalin signed a joint pact to invade and divide Poland.

The rest of this section is devoted solely to Communism because, while Nazism is dead, it is the totalitarianism that continues.

To make an omelette you have to break eggs.

Vladimir Ilich Lenin
(justifying murders of
anti-Communists)

One cannot make an omelette without breaking eggs – but it is amazing how many eggs one can break without making a decent omelette.

Charles Issawi
(Issawi's Laws of Social Action)

None of the evils that totalitarianism, defined by the single party and the suppression of all opposition, claims to remedy, is worse than totalitarianism itself.

Albert Camus
("Socialism of the Gallows")

Authoritarian socialism has failed almost everywhere, but you will not find a single Marxist who will say that it has failed because it was wrong or impractical. He will say it has failed because nobody went far enough with it. So failure never proves that a myth was wrong.

Jean François Revel

When it comes time to hang the capitalists they will compete with each other to sell us the rope at a lower price.

Vladimir Ilich Lenin

When they bury us in the ground alive...please do not send them shovels. Please do not send them the latest earth-moving equipment.

Alexander Solzhenitsyn
(Warning to the West)
Solzhenitsyn was addressing
the American corporations which
applied in the early 1970s to the
U.S. government for permission
to sell surveillance and
eavesdropping devices to the KGB.

The Russian people's...worst misfortune was his birth, the next worse his death.

Winston Churchill
(The World Crisis)
Churchill was writing of
Lenin, who died in 1924, and
was succeeded by Stalin, who
murdered over 18 million people
in the large prison camps
known as the Gulag Archipelago.

The problem with socialism is socialism. The problem with capitalism is capitalists.

Winston Churchill

The inherent vice of capitalism is the unequal sharing of blessings: the inherent virtue of socialism is the equal sharing of misery.

Winston Churchill

That Communism has been an economic failure is certainly obvious to any Westerner who has visited a Communist country. The simplest Western conveniences, such as ballpoint pens and chewing gum, are deeply coveted. But the completeness of the Communist economic failure is rarely appreciated. In *The Totalitarian Temptation,* Jean François Revel offers some comparative data on the United States and the Soviet economies. In 1900, Russian agriculture was more productive than American agriculture. In the late 1970s, after more than sixty years of Communist rule, a third of the Soviet work force was still employed in agriculture, and the country produced considerably less food than its 242 million citizens required. In the United States, less than 4 percent of the work force were farmers, and they not only met the food needs of the country, they also exported to numerous other countries – including the Soviet Union.

The failure of Communist economies is not restricted to the Soviet Union. Taiwan, for instance, is much more prosperous than Communist mainland China. In *Chinese Shadows,* Simon Leys tells the story of a Chinese peasant who escaped to Hong Kong in the early 1960s and was interviewed there. "The interviewer was asking him what he knew about other countries. When asked, 'What do you know about Yugoslavia?' the peasant, painstaking and placid, answered, 'It is a pseudosocialist country run by revisionist hyenas in the pay of American capitalism.' Somewhat later, the interviewer asked: 'If you could choose, where would you wish to live?' 'Well, in Yugoslavia, for example.' 'Why?' 'It seems that in pseudosocialist countries run by revisionist hyenas in the pay of American capitalism, oil and cotton cloth are not rationed'."

The whole country has a fixation on shoes. Moscow is the only city where, if Marilyn Monroe walked down the street with nothing on but a pair of shoes, people would stare at her feet first.

John Gunther
(Inside Russia Today)

Under capitalism man exploits man. Under Communism it's just the opposite.

Moscow dissident joke

In the West the future is always changing. In the Soviet Union the future remains the same. It's the past that is always changing.

Moscow dissident joke

Both the Soviet Union and the United States have freedom of speech. The only difference is that the United States has freedom after speech.

Moscow dissident joke

In the Soviet Union, political jokes are no laughing matter. As the Russian satirist **Nikolai Gogol** noted over a century ago, "Even he who fears nothing fears laughter." Alexander Solzhenitsyn spent years in the Gulag because of a joking reference he made about Stalin in a letter to a friend.

The funniest dissident joke I know is one I heard from Robert Toth, a *Los Angeles Times* correspondent who was expelled from Russia on charges of having served as Anatoly Shcharansky's CIA connection. Toth heard this joke from Jewish dissidents in Moscow:

In the early 1970s, Brezhnev announces that he will make a state visit to Poland. He wants to bring the Polish people a gift from the Soviet people and concludes that the most fitting present would be a painting of Lenin, the god of Soviet Communism, visiting Poland. But Lenin never was in Poland, and when the Union of Socialist Artists is assigned the task of producing the painting they cannot come up with anything. The visit is drawing near and the leadership is growing desperate. They finally decide to approach Rabinowitz, a talented artist, but a dissident.

"If you make this painting of Lenin in Poland for the Motherland," they tell him, "you will get work and a beautiful apartment. We will completely forget about your dissident activities."

Rabinowitz consents. Three weeks later the supreme leadership of the Soviet Union, accompanied by Brezhnev, file into a room where Rabinowitz stands next to a canvas covered by a drop cloth.

"Show us the painting," Brezhnev commands.

Rabinowitz removes the cloth and the assemblage gasps. The painting shows a man in bed with a woman.

"Who is that man?" Brezhnev asks indignantly.

"Trotsky," Rabinowitz responds.

"And who is that woman?"

"Krupsaya, Lenin's wife."

"And where is Lenin?" Brezhnev explodes.

"Lenin's in Poland."

Better Red than dead.

> Popularized by **Bertrand Russell**
> in the 1950s, the expression
> became a slogan of pacifist
> and antinuclear groups.

Better to be dead than a scoundrel.

> **Alexander Solzhenitsyn**
> *(Warning to the West)*

FANATICISM

A fanatic is a man who does what he thinks the Lord would do if he knew the facts of the case.

Finley Peter Dunne
(American humorist)

It is easier to devote one's life to fanaticism.... The Flat Earth society is, after all, more committed to its flatness than I am to its roundness.

Lionel Blue
(A Backdoor to Heaven)

Fanaticism consists in redoubling your effort when you have forgotten your aim.

George Santayana

A fanatic is one who can't change his mind and won't change the subject.

Winston Churchill

The tendency to claim God as an ally for our partisan values and ends is... the source of all religious fanaticism.

Reinhold Niebuhr

Faith in a holy cause is to a considerable extent a substitute for the lost faith in ourselves. The less justified a man is in claiming excellence for his own self, the more ready is he to claim all excellence for his nation, his religion, his race or his holy cause.

Eric Hoffer
(The True Believer)

The evil is not what they [extremists] say about their cause, but what they say about their opponents.

Robert F. Kennedy

Brooks Hays, an Arkansas congressman, told of a temperance candidate, a fanatic on the subject of liquor, who primly declared in a speech, "I would rather commit adultery than drink a glass of beer." A heckler called out, "Who wouldn't?"

CRIME AND PUNISHMENT

The long and distressing controversy over capital punishment is very unfair to anyone meditating murder.

Geoffrey Fisher
(Archbishop of Canterbury)

The unbeliever cannot keep from thinking that men who have set at the center of their faith the staggering victim of a judicial error ought at least to hesitate before committing legal murder.

Albert Camus
("Reflections on the Guillotine")

Punishment And Deterrence

To spare the ravening leopard is an act of injustice to the sheep.

Persian proverb

When you repay kindness with kindness, then the people are encouraged to do good. When you repay evil with evil, then people are warned from doing bad.

Lin Yutang
(The Wisdom of Confucius)

The assertion that punishment does not deter runs contrary to the common sense of the common man, and is perhaps, for that reason, a tenet fiercely held by a number of social scientists.

Robert Bork
(Solicitor General of
the United States)

Criminal Lawyers

You can't earn a living defending innocent people.

Maurice Nadjari
(New York City
special prosecutor)

Get them off anyway you can.

William Kunstler
Kunstler served as chief defense
lawyer for the "Chicago 8," and
is still today one of the leading
radical lawyers in the United States.

William Kunstler, so concerned with his client's rights, is extraordinarily unconcerned with the rights of people living in Communist countries. He has declared elsewhere: "I do not believe in public attacks on socialist countries where violations of human rights may occur" (quoted by Nat Hentoff in *The Village Voice*, May 28, 1979). Consequently, he attacked Joan Baez for her public protest against genocide in Cambodia, and Alan Dershowitz for his opposition to the Soviet kangaroo court that sentenced Jewish dissident Anatoly Shcharansky to thirteen years in prison (see Alan Dershowitz, *The Best Defense*).

The courtroom oath – "to tell the truth, the whole truth and nothing but the truth" – is applicable only to witnesses. Defense attorneys, prosecutors and judges don't take this oath – they couldn't. Indeed, it is fair to say that the American justice system is built on a foundation of *not* telling the whole truth.

Alan Dershowitz
(The Best Defense)

A jury consists of twelve persons chosen to decide who has the better lawyer.

Robert Frost

Manipulating The Judicial System

In England. . . persons detected in espionage on behalf of the Soviet Union are instructed. . . to plead guilty. . . . In the United States, where legal proceedings are likely to be prolonged and confused, and all sorts of considerations may prevent the truth from appearing, it is worthwhile putting up a plea of not guilty, no matter how absurd this may be in view of the real facts.

George Will
(in his syndicated column,
March 20, 1978; citing a Soviet
agent quoted in Rebecca West's
The New Meaning of Treason)

Miscellaneous

If Robert Kennedy were alive today, he would not countenance singling me out for this kind of treatment.

Sirhan Sirhan
(Robert Kennedy's murderer,
arguing for parole from his
life sentence at California's
Soledad prison, 1983)

Sirhan's *chutzpah* reminds me of the joke about the man who murdered both his parents and then asked the court to treat him leniently because he was an orphan.

An Irish attorney was making the best of a rather shaky case when the judge interrupted him on a point of law. "Surely," he asked, "your clients are aware of the doctrine *da minimis not curat lex?*" "I assure you, my lord," came the suave reply, "that in the remote. . . hamlet where my clients have their humble abode, it forms the sole topic of conversation."

Walter Bryan
(The Improbable Irish)

HUNTING

When a man wants to murder a tiger, he calls it sport; when a tiger wants to murder him, he calls it ferocity.

George Bernard Shaw

Hi, handsome hunting man
Fire your little gun
Bang! Now the animal
is dead and dumb and done
Nevermore to peep again,
creep again, leap again
Eat or sleep or drink again
Oh, what fun!

Walter De La Mare
(Hi)

It is very strange and melancholy that the paucity of human pleasures should persuade us ever to call hunting one of them.

Samuel Johnson

The English country gentleman galloping after a fox – the unspeakable in full pursuit of the uneatable.

Oscar Wilde
(A Woman of No Importance)

Hunting is so popular in the United States that the American Congress is unable to pass an effective law limiting civilian access to guns because of National Rifle Association lobbying against the bill. Though overwhelming evidence suggests that a gun-control law would lower the number of murders in the U.S., many hunters oppose this legislation fearing their access to weapons might be limited.

The late Sen Hubert Humphrey did little to help gun-control advocates with his unintentionally funny response to Sara Jane Moore's narrowly averted assassination attempt on President Ford in 1975: "There are too many guns in the hands of people who don't know how to use them."

When a Jew says he's going hunting to amuse himself, he lies.
Walter Rathenau
(Finance Minister in the
Weimar Republic, who was
assassinated by right-wing
extremists in 1922)

Rathenau, himself a Jew, was referring to the well-known Jewish antipathy to hunting. Different explanations have been offered for this, the most cogent being that biblical and Talmudic law forbids the eating of any animal not killed instantly, with a single stroke. Since their earliest history, Jews were almost never hunters. But today, the distaste for hunting persists even among nonreligious Jews. The reasons for this, both psychological and moral, were best articulated more than a century ago by the Jewish-born German poet **Heinrich Heine:** "My ancestors did not belong to the hunters so much as to the hunted, and the idea of attacking the descendants of those who were our comrades in misery goes against my grain."

RACISM

It is a great shock at the age of five or six to find that in a world of Gary Coopers you are the Indian.

James Baldwin

I swear to the Lord
I still can't see
Why democracy means
Everybody but me.

Langston Hughes

Here lies the body of John Jack, a native of Africa . . .
Though born in a land of slavery
He was born free
Though he lived in a land of liberty
He lived a slave.

Epitaph for John Jack
John Jack was an American
slave who died in 1772.

"Well, sir, I can prove from the Bible that slavery [of Blacks] is right." "Ah!" replied I, "that is a precious book – the rule of conduct. I have always supposed that its spirit was directly opposed to everything in the shape of fraud and oppression. However, sir, I should be glad to hear your text." He somewhat hesitatingly muttered out, "Ham – Noah's curse, you know." "O sir, you build on a very slender foundation. Granting, even, what remains to be proved, that the Africans are the descendants of Ham, Noah's curse was a *prediction* of future servitude, and not an *injunction* to oppress. Pray, sir, is it a careful desire to fulfill the Scriptures, or to make money, that induces you to hold your fellowman in bondage?"

Abolitionist William Lloyd Garrison
(in the magazine *The Liberator*, 1831)

While the Bible, written 3,000 years ago, did allow for slavery, it hedged it with so many restrictions that it was very different from the slavery practiced in the American South. The most important differences were that murdering a slave was a capital offense (Exodus 21:20), while a master who punished a slave so that he lost a limb, or even a tooth, had to set him free (Exodus 21:26-27). It was also forbidden to return a runaway slave to his master (Deuteronomy 23:16). All these biblical laws were ignored in the South. There are few more hideous examples of religious hypocrisy than the attempts by some nineteenth-century Southerners to use the Bible to justify their practice of slavery.

I do not care if half the league strikes. Those who do will encounter quick retribution. All will be suspended, and I don't care if it wrecks the National League for five years. This is the United States of America and one citizen has as much right to play as another. The National League will go down the line with Robinson whatever the consequences.

Ford Frick
(Commissioner of the National Baseball League, 1947) Frick's statement was directed at the St. Louis Cardinals, who planned to strike when Jackie Robinson

and the Dodgers came to play them;
it is quoted in Roger Kahn's *The Boys
of Summer.* Kahn notes that after Frick's
statement, "Robinson's road, although
still steep, led from thicket to clearing."

For God's sake, after you beat a white opponent, don't smile.
(Manager's advice to Heavyweight Boxing
Champion Joe Louis in the 1930s)

She even thinks that up in heaven
Her class lies late and snores
While poor black cherubs rise at seven
To do celestial chores.

Countee Cullen
(writing of a white woman's
thoughts about black servants)

What happens to a dream deferred?
Does it dry up like a raisin in the sun –
Or fester like a sore – and then run!
Does it stink like rotten meat?
Or crust and sugar over – like a syrupy sweet?
Maybe it just sags
Like a heavy load.
Or does it explode?

Langston Hughes

There are no "white" or "colored" signs in the foxholes or grave-
yards of battles.

John F. Kennedy
(civil rights message to
Congress, January 19, 1963)

Infamous Quotes

[A black person] has no rights which a white man need respect.

Chief Justice Roger Taney,
in the Supreme Court decision on the
Dred Scot case, 1857, which gave
Southerners the right to recover runaway
slaves from free states. To extricate
itself from this immoral mess, the Court
would have had to violate the doctrine
of separation of Church and State and
rely on the 3,000 year-old biblical
injunction: "You shall not return a
runaway slave who seeks refuge with
you to his master" [Deuteronomy 23:16].

The action of President [Theodore] Roosevelt in entertaining that Negro, Booker T. Washington, will necessitate our killing a thousand Negroes in the South before they learn their place again.

Sen. Benjamin R. Tillman
of South Carolina,
after Booker T. Washington had
dined at the White House in 1901.

Why would we have different races if God meant us to be alike and associate with each other?

Gov. Lester Maddox of Georgia

American Indians

When asked by an anthropologist what the Indians called America before the white men came, an Indian said simply, "Ours."

Vine Deloria, Jr.

Mrs. Ogden Reid of *The New York Herald Tribune* once attacked Churchill for his colonialist views on India. "The Indians," she charged, "have suffered years under British oppression." Churchill replied: "Before we proceed further let us get one thing clear. Are we talking about the Indians in India who have multiplied alarmingly under benevolent British rule, or are we talking about the Indians in America who, I understand, are now almost extinct.

James Hume
(Churchill)

They [the white men] made us many promises, more than I can remember, but they never kept but one: they promised to take our land and they took it.

Anonymous Indian
(quoted in Dee Brown's
Bury My Heart at Wounded Knee)

Infamous Quotes

To Lem S. Frame who during his life shot eighty-nine Indians, whom the Lord delivered into his hands, and who was looking forward to making up his hundred before the end of the year, when he fell asleep in Jesus, at his house at Hawk's Ferry, March 2, 1843.

Tombstone inscription
(in Gyles Brandreth's
The Last Word)

The only good Indians I ever saw were dead.
Gen. Philip Sheridan

Sheridan made this comment to an Indian brave, Tosawi, who led a delegation of surrendering Indians, who were attacked without provocation. When Tosawi met Sheridan he said in broken English, "Tosawi, good Indian." Sheridan responded with the above. **Dee Brown** writes in *Bury My Heart At Wounded Knee*: "Lieutenant Charles Nordstrom who was present, remembered the words and passed them on, until in time they were honed into an American aphorism, 'The only good Indian is a dead one'." Subsequent bigots of all persuasions have applied Sheridan's quote to whichever group they hated.

I don't feel we did wrong in taking this great country away from them. There were great numbers of people who needed new land, and the Indians were selfishly trying to keep it for themselves.

John Wayne
(in a *Playboy* interview,
May, 1971)

I don't go so far as to think that the only good Indians are dead Indians, but I believe nine out of every ten are, and I shouldn't inquire too closely into the case of the tenth. The most vicious cowboy has more moral principle than the average Indian.

Theodore Roosevelt
(The Winning of the West,
1889-1896)

PREJUDICE

Whenever someone speaks with prejudice against a group –
Catholics, Jews, Italians, Negroes – someone else usually comes
up with a classic line of defense: "Look at Einstein!" "Look at
Carver!" "Look at Toscanini!" So, of course, Catholics (or Jews, or
Italians, or Negroes) must be all right.

They mean well, these defenders. But their approach is wrong. It
is even bad. What a minority group wants is not the right to have
geniuses among them but the right to have fools and scoundrels
without being condemned as a group.

Agnes Elizabeth Benedict

Infidel – in New York, one who does not believe in the Christian
religion; in Constantinople, one who does.

Ambrose Bierce
(A Cynic's Dictionary)

There are only two ways to be quite unprejudiced and impartial.
One is to be completely ignorant. The other is to be completely
indifferent.

Charles Curtis
(A Commonplace Book)

Never try to reason the prejudice out of a man. It was not reasoned
into him, and cannot be reasoned out.

Sydney Smith
(English clergyman and essayist;
1771-1845)

Joseph Telushkin

Prejudgments become prejudices only if they are not reversible when exposed to new knowledge.

Gordon Allport
(The Nature of Prejudice)

I would put it another way: since we all have prejudices, how do we know if our prejudice is a dangerous one? If we are always looking for evidence to support it, and are happy when we find it. But if we are happier when we find evidence disputing our prejudice, then it is not dangerous.

ANTISEMITISM

An antisemite is a person who hates Jews more than is absolutely necessary.

Jewish proverb

The world is divided into two groups of nations – those that want to expel the Jews and those that do not want to receive them.

Chaim Weizmann
(in the late 1930s)
It was this worldwide
unwillingness to offer refuge
to the Jews that convinced
Hitler he had international
support for his anti-Jewish acts.

Not long ago I was reading the Sermon on the Mount with a rabbi. At nearly every verse he showed me very similar passages in the Hebrew Bible and Talmud. When we reached the words, "Turn the other cheek," he did not say this too is in the Talmud, but asked with a smile, "Do the Christians obey this command?" I had nothing to say in reply, especially as at that particular time, Christians, far from turning the other cheek, were smiting the Jews on both cheeks.

Leo Tolstoy
(My Religion)

If my theory of relativity is proven successful, Germany will claim me as a German and France will declare that I am a citizen of the world. If my theory should prove to be untrue, then France will say I am a German, and Germany will say I am a Jew.

Albert Einstein

What a shame it is that they should be more miserable under Christian princes than their ancestors were under Pharaoh.

Pope Innocent IV
(Letter in Defense of the Jews, 1247)
The Pope's noble declaration was
perhaps an apology for his namesake
Pope Innocent III who had written
in 1208: "The Jews, against whom
the blood of Jesus calls out. . .
must remain vagabonds upon the
earth, until their faces be
covered with shame and they seek
the name of Jesus Christ the Lord."

They should have come out with a very simple statement: we have been guilty of antisemitism for two thousand years. Forgive us.

Edward Keating

Keating, a Catholic writer, was referring to Vatican II's declaration that not all Jews of Jesus' time, nor Jews of subsequent generations, were to be held guilty for his crucifixion. Although the declaration both irritated and pleased the Jewish community (with the pleasure predominating, of course), **Pope John XXIII**, who was the moving force behind the declaration, *did* want to apologize to the Jews. Shortly before his death he composed this prayer:

"We realize now that many, many centuries of blindness have dimmed our eyes, so that we no longer see the beauty of Thy Chosen People and no longer recognize in their faces the features of our first-born brother. We realize that our brows are branded with the mark of Cain. Centuries long has Abel lain in blood and tears, because we had forgotten Thy love. Forgive us the curse which we unjustly laid on the name of the Jews. Forgive us, that with our curse, we crucified Thee a second time."

Antisemitism is, unfortunately, not only a feeling which all Gentiles at times feel, but also, and this is what matters, a feeling of which the majority of them are not ashamed.

W. H. Auden

In the warmest of hearts there is a cold spot for the Jews.

Irving Howe

Since my little daughter is only half-Jewish, would it be all right if she went into the pool only up to her waist?

Groucho Marx
(in a letter to a country
club that barred his daughter
from membership)

Infamous Quotes

Jewish priests have always sacrificed human victims with their sacred hands.

Voltaire
(1770 appendix to his
entry on the Jews in his
Dictionnaire Philosophique)
This quote and other libels
by the most prominent thinker of
the Enlightenment did much to
advance modern antisemitism.

Grant them civil rights? I see no other way of doing this except to cut off all their heads on one night and substitute other heads without a single Jewish thought in them.

Johann Fichte
(German Enlightenment leader)

Money is the jealous God of Israel before whom no other gods are allowed to stand.

Karl Marx
(The Jewish Question)
Marx was born to a Jewish family
in Germany and was converted to
Christianity at the age of six.
According to Hitler, this essay
by Marx helped develop his own
thinking about the Jews.

The Jew came into our gay world and spoiled everything with his ominous concept of sin, with his Law and his Cross.

Houston Stewart Chamberlain

(author of *Foundations of the Nineteenth Century*)
Published at the turn of the century, Chamberlain's racial interpretation of history became an international best-seller and exerted tremendous influence throughout the Western world, particularly in Germany. Sigmund Freud later responded to Chamberlain and similar antisemites in *Moses and Monotheism:* "The hatred for Judaism," he wrote, "is at bottom hatred for Christianity."

It's their own bloody fault – they should have left God alone.

Hilaire Belloc

The belief that Jesus Christ was God and that the Jews killed him, intensified antisemitism. Fear lay at the bottom of this hatred, because, if the Jews had killed God, it meant that their powers were both superhuman and demonic.

While this may be the psychological basis of antisemitism, it is of course historically incorrect. Crucifixion was the Roman punishment for rebels. Jesus was one of between 50,000 and 100,000 Jews crucified as anti-Roman rebels in the first century. Historian **Hyam Maccoby** has written: "The cross became as much a symbol of Roman oppression as nowadays the gas chamber is a symbol of German Nazi oppression. . . . Associating the guilt of the cross with the Jews rather than the Romans is comparable to branding the Jewish victims. . . with the guilt of using gas chambers instead of suffering from them" (*Revolution in Judaea*, p. 36).

When you baptize a Jew hold his head under water for five minutes.

Bulgarian proverb

We are fighting against the most ancient curse that humanity has brought upon itself. Against the so-called Ten Commandments, against them we are fighting.

Adolf Hitler
(in conversation with
Herman Rauschning)

Fifteen-year-old **Anne Frank,** though unfamiliar with Hitler's comment, intuitively understood the basis of his hatred. "Who knows, it might even be our religion from which the world and all peoples learn good, and for that reason and that reason only do we now suffer" (*The Diary of a Young Girl,* April 11, 1944).

THE BEST IS THE ENEMY OF THE BETTER – AGAINST UTOPIANISM

The calf and the lion shall lie down together but the calf won't get any sleep.

Woody Allen

Perhaps we cannot prevent this world from being a world in which children are tortured. But we can reduce the number of tortured children.

Albert Camus
("The Unbeliever and Christians")

It is not your obligation to complete the work [of perfecting the world], but neither are you free from doing all you can.

Talmud
(Ethics of the Fathers, 2:21)

An acre in Middlesex is better than a principality in Utopia.

Thomas Macaulay
(Francis Bacon)

St. Francis of Assisi was hoeing his garden when he was asked what he would do if he was suddenly informed that he would die at sunset that night. "I should finish hoeing my garden," he said.

Rabbi Yohanan ben Zakkai used to say: "If there is a plant in your hand when they say to you, 'Behold, the Messiah has come!' go and plant the plant, and afterwards go out and greet him.

Talmud
(The Fathers of Rabbi Nathan)
The first-century Rabbi Yohanan was
registering his profound mistrust of
the frequent Messiahs and messianic
movements that rose during his lifetime,
claiming to redeem men and end history.

In 1951, **Winston Churchill** went on a trip visiting NATO defenses. Enroute to Cyprus he asked Minister of Defense Harold McMillan what kind of man Archbishop Makarios, the head of Cyprus, was. "Is he one of those priestly ascetics concerned only with spiritual things, or one of those crafty prelates concerned with temporal gain?"

"Regrettably," answered McMillan, "the archbishop seems to be one of the latter."

"Good," said Churchill. "He is one of our kind and we can work together."

My late grandfather, Rabbi Nissen Telushkin, was a rabbi for many years in a small town in Russia. He told me that the Jews there feared most a police chief who was an idealist. "If he was an idealist, then when the order came to make a pogrom, there was nothing we could do to stop him. But if he was corrupt, then we could always bribe him to do what was right."

You don't have to be an angel in order to be a saint.

Albert Schweitzer

The best is the enemy of the good.

Voltaire
("Art Dramatique," in
Dictionnaire Philosophique)

The best is the enemy of the better.

Unknown

WRITING AND READING

Writing

Winston Churchill confided to friends that of one thing he was certain: history would treat him well. "What makes you so sure?" they asked. "Because I intend to write it," answered the author-to-be of a six-volume history of World War II.

Anybody who believes you can't change history has never tried to write his memoirs.

Unknown
(Possibly a reformulation
of **Samuel Butler**'s dictum,
"God cannot alter the past
but historians can.")

Just how difficult it is to write biography can be reckoned by anybody who sits down and considers just how many people know the real truth about his or her love affairs.

Rebecca West

In a good play everyone is in the right.

Friedrich Hebbel

There are books showing men how to succeed in everything: they are written by men who cannot even succeed in writing books.

G. K. Chesterton

Writing is one of the easiest things: erasing is one of the hardest.

Rabbi Israel Salanter

This nineteenth-century Eastern European rabbi is also reputed to have said: "Ninety percent of what is thought shouldn't be said; ninety percent of what is said shouldn't be written; ninety percent of what is written shouldn't be published; ninety percent of what is published shouldn't be read; ninety percent of what is read shouldn't be remembered."

The reason why so few good books are written is that so few people who can write know anything.

Walter Bagehot
(Literary Studies)

An appealing character strives against great odds to attain a worthwhile goal. That's pretty much the formula for all fiction.

Dan Greenburg
(in his book
What Do Women Want;
quoting an unnamed writer at
the *Saturday Evening Post*)

Greenburg notes that as long as one of these elements is strongly present, the other two can be somewhat compromised. "In *The Day of the Jackal* [by Frederick Forsythe] the main character was a professional killer and not a very likable fellow. And his goal, the assassination of de Gaulle, wasn't what you might call worthwhile. But still there were great odds, and the author had researched and paced his story so well that. . . you wanted the assassin in some horrible way to succeed and kill de Gaulle, even though you knew he couldn't."

The novelist, afraid his ideas may be foolish, slyly puts them in the mouth of some other fool, and reserves the right to disavow them.

Diane Johnson

The written word is no mirror of the writer's character. . . . The amateur, though a selfless angel, may show himself a pompous ass, while the professional, a monster of ego, can convince you in a phrase that he has the innocence of a child.

Louis Auchincloss
(The Rector of Justin)

Only a mediocre writer is always at his best.

W. Somerset Maugham
(The Summing Up)

Asking a working writer what he thinks about critics is like asking a lamppost how it feels about dogs.

Christopher Hampton

I have never met an author who admitted that people did not buy his book because it was dull.

W. Somerset Maugham

Reading

It is not true that we have only one life to live; if we can read we can live as many more lives and as many kinds as we wish.

Sen. S. I. Hayakawa

The man who does not read good books has no advantage over the man who can't read them.

Mark Twain

When you reread a classic you do not see more in the book than you did before; you see more in *you* than there was before.

Clifton Fadiman
(Any Number Can Play)

A classic is something that everybody wants to have read and nobody wants to read.

Mark Twain
("The Disappearance of Literature")

A man ought to read just as inclination leads him; for what he reads as a task will do him little good. A young man should read five hours in a day and so may acquire a great deal of knowledge.

Samuel Johnson

The oldest books are still only just out to those who have not read them.

Samuel Butler

REASON GONE MAD:
THE WORLD OF THE ABSURD

More than at any time in history mankind faces a crossroads. One path leads to despair and utter hopelessness, the other to total extinction. Let us pray that we have the wisdom to choose correctly.
Woody Allen

The priest was saying, "Every man in this parish must die one day." A little man was laughing. Finally the priest asked him, "And why are you laughing?" "I'm not from this parish," the little man responded.

Pat O'Brien
(American actor)

Anybody who looks like their passport photo is too sick to travel.
Will Kommen
(quoted in Laurence S. Peter's
Peter's Quotations)

Well if I called the wrong number why did you answer the phone?
James Thurber

When you are awakened by a ringing phone and asked, "Oh, did I wake you up?" the right answer is, "No, I was just getting up to answer the phone."

Tell us your phobias and we will tell you what you are afraid of.

Robert Benchley

In my youth I wanted to be a great pantomimist but I found I had nothing to say.

Victor Borge

In an age when the fashion is to be in love with yourself, confessing to being in love with somebody else is an admission of unfaithfulness to one's beloved.

Russell Baker

We hope that when the insects take over the world they will remember with gratitude how we took them along on all our picnics.

Bill Vaughan

The Jewish position on abortion is that a fetus is a fetus until it gets out of medical school.

Unknown
(quoted in Robert Byrne's
The 637 Best Things Ever Said)

The time is at hand when the wearing of a prayer shawl and skull cap will not bar a man from the White House – unless, of course, the man is Jewish.

Wallace Markfield
(You Could Live if They Let You)

Toots Shor Restaurant is so crowded nobody goes there anymore.

Yogi Berra
The great Yankee catcher
also said, "You can observe
a lot by just watching."

Here lies
Lester Moore
Four slugs
From a .44
No Les
No more

Arizona tombstone inscription
(reported by Gyles Brandreth in
The Last Word)

Anybody who goes to see a psychiatrist ought to have his head examined.

Samuel Goldwyn

I don't want any yes men around me. I want everyone to tell me the truth – even though it costs him his job.

Samuel Goldwyn

Groucho Marx was dragged to a séance with a medium, the Great Nairobi, who was arousing tremendous enthusiasm in Hollywood. During the evening, the all-knowing medium communicated with various dead relatives of those present, and gave a lot of advice. At midnight she announced that there was time for one last question: "What's the capital of North Dakota?" Groucho asked.

Leo Rosten writes of two of his encounters with Groucho's wit: Once in a restaurant, after studying the menu thoughtfully, Groucho asked the waitress, "Do you have frog's legs?"

"I don't think so," she said.

"That's the wrong answer," mourned Groucho. "You should have said, 'No, it's my rheumatism makes me walk this way'."

On another occasion, as he was leaving Marx's house, Rosten said: "I'd like to say good-bye to your wife." Groucho responded: "Who wouldn't?"

Leo Rosten
*(People I Have Loved
Known or Admired)*

"Mr. President: Has government been lacking in courage and boldness in facing up to the recession?"

President Dwight D. Eisenhower: "Listen, there is no courage or any extra courage that I know of to find out the right thing to do. Now it is not only necessary to do the right thing, but to do it in the right way and the only problem you have is what is the right way to do it. That is the problem. But this economy of ours is not so simple that it obeys to the opinion or bias or pronouncements of any particular individual, even to the President. This is an economy that is made up of 173 million people and it reflects their desires: they're ready to buy, they're ready to spend, it is a thing that is too complex and too big to be affected adversely or advantageously just by a few words or any particular – say a little this and that, or even a panacea so alleged.

**Question and answer at a
Presidential press conference**
(quoted in Robert Byrne's
The 637 Best Things Ever Said)

Jeffrey Hart, an Eisenhower admirer, argues that the president's "press-conference garbled syntax served a deliberate purpose. . . . Eisenhower often confused his opponents and kept his options open by beclouding the issue" (Jeffrey Hart, *When the Going Was Good*). Though few would dispute that statements such as the above "confused his opponents," they were not the only ones confused – his supporters were, too.

They have vilified me, they have crucified me, they have even criticized me.

> **Mayor Richard Daley** of Chicago
> (responding to attacks on his
> handling of protests at the 1968
> Democratic National Convention)

A 1973 issue of *World Magazine* contained the following classified ad: "If you bought our course 'How to Fly Solo in 6 Easy Lessons' we apologize for any inconvenience caused by our failure to include the last chapter, entitled 'How to Land Your Plane Safely.' Send us your name and address and we will send you the last chapter posthaste. Requests by estates also honored.

> (quoted in Don Atyeo's
> and Jonathon Green's
> book *Don't Quote Me*)

CUSTOMERS GIVING ORDERS WILL BE SWIFTLY EXECUTED

> **Sign on tailor shop in
> Kowloon, Hong Kong**
> (quoted in Leo Rosten's
> *The 3:10 to Anywhere*)

Nothing worth noting.

> Diary entry of **Louis XVI**
> for July 14, 1789, the day
> the Bastille was stormed.

INFAMOUS QUOTATIONS

People ask me who my heroes are. I have only one – Hitler.
Nguyen Cao My
(Premier of South Vietnam;
in an interview in the *London
Sunday Mirror,* July 4, 1965)

I do not consider Hitler to be as bad as he is depicted. He is showing an ability that is amazing and he seems to be gaining his victories without much bloodshed.
Mahatma Gandhi
(remark to Rajkumari Amrit,
May, 1940; quoted in
Robert Payne's *The Life and
Death of Mahatma Gandhi*)

The outer world would do well to accept the evidence of German good will and seek by all possible means to meet it and justify it.
Walter Lippmann
(in his syndicated newspaper
column, May 18, 1933, praising
Hitler for a speech in which
the Führer denounced war)
Lippmann, the most famous
columnist of his time, was
an assimilated Jew, and his
early, sympathetic assessments
of Hitler so infuriated his close
friend, Felix Frankfurter, that for
years the two did not speak.

I was an idealist.

Adolf Eichmann
(July 12, 1961, before he
was executed by the state of
Israel for his role in
murdering 6 million Jews)

To choose one's victim, to prepare one's plans minutely, to slake an implacable vengeance and then to go to bed . . . there is nothing sweeter in the world.

Joseph Stalin
(to friend and later victim
Felix Dzerzhinsky, founder and
chief of the Soviet secret police)

A child would like to sit in his lap and a dog would sidle up to him.

Joseph Davies
(the first American ambassador to
the U.S.S.R. describing Stalin in
his memoir, *Mission to Moscow*)
Years later it was revealed that
Stalin had authorized the continuous
sale of valuable Soviet art to Davies
at extraordinarily low prices – in effect
bribing him to file pro-Stalin reports
with the U.S. State Department
[see Paul Johnson, *Modern Times*].

Political power grows out of the barrel of a gun.

Mao Tse-Tung
(Quotations of Chairman Mao)

So well-known and effective is the Soviet method of remaking human beings that criminals occasionally now apply to be admitted.

Anna Louise Strong
(Western Communist leader, on
Stalin's prison camps in the 1930s)

After all, in our prisons, too, there are hundreds, perhaps even thousands of people I would call political prisoners.

Andrew Young
(American Ambassador to the
United Nations, July, 1978)
Young was undercutting
President Carter's denunciation of
the conviction of Russian dissident
Anatoly Shcharansky by the Soviet
Union as an attack on every human
being who believes in freedom.

I cannot tolerate bigots. They are all so obstinate, so opinionated.

Sen. Joseph McCarthy

The first part of the Yippie program, you know, is to kill your parents. And I mean that quite seriously. Because until you're prepared to kill your parents, you're not really prepared to change the country, because our parents are our first oppressors.

Jerry Rubin

What are the lives of a million men to me!

Napoleon Bonaparte

Nature intended women to be our slaves...they are our property ...they belong to us just as a tree that bears fruit to a gardener. What a mad idea to demand equality for women!... Women are nothing but machines for producing children.

Napoleon Bonaparte

Bishop **Fulton Sheen** told the following story on the "Merv Griffin Show" (November 18, 1969): "Pope John was visiting a prison and he came across a man who had killed his wife. John said to him, 'You know, I was never married, but if I had been I might have killed my wife too'."

Sooner murder an infant in its cradle than nurse unacted desires.

William Blake

I am the divine way, the torch that lights the dark. There is no god but Ali Solih.

Ali Solih
(leader of the African country
Comoros from 1976 to 1978)

In his book *The Africans*, **David Lamb** describes the rape, terror and murder that ensued under Solih's regime, noting that "it was as though Los Angeles had made Charles Manson mayor." This modern tyrant is reminiscent of those Roman emperors who saw themselves as divine. For example, in 39 E.C., Caligula declared himself to be god and decreed that his statue be erected in every temple in the Roman Empire and sacrifices brought before it. When Jews in Palestine resisted this edict, he ordered their temple destroyed. Only his death, shortly thereafter, cancelled the edict.

Question: Do you consider ten dollars a week enough for a long-shoreman with a family to support?

J. Pierpont Morgan: If that's all he can get, and he takes it, I should say it's enough.

Even if he were mediocre, there are a lot of mediocre judges and people and lawyers, and they are entitled to a little representation, aren't they?

Sen. Roman Hruska
(defending Nixon's Supreme Court
nomination of G. Harrold Carswell
in 1970) Carswell's reaction to
Hruska's ringing declaration
of support is not known.

MISCELLANEOUS QUOTES
ON 87 SUBJECTS

A MISCELLANY

Accuracy: Every man has a right to his own opinion. But no man has a right to be wrong in his facts.

Bernard Baruch

Acting: In the car I wonder if I am having a nervous breakdown. And if so, can I give it artistic expression?

Liv Ullmann
(in her autobiographical
work *Changing*)

Actions: What you do speaks so loud that I cannot hear what you say.

Ralph Waldo Emerson

Ambitiousness: A man wants to be a leader and a scholar overnight, and to sleep that night as well.

Rabbi Yaizel of Navorodok

Ancestry: A person who always brags about his ancestors is like a potato – the best part of him is underground.

Yiddish proverb

Anger: Think when you are enraged at anyone, what would probably become your sentiments should he die during the dispute.

William Shenstone

Arguments: You can disagree with a man's position as much as you want – *after* you have been able to state it, to his satisfaction.

J. Irwin Miller

Art: Picasso refused to sign three of his paintings which he declared to be fakes. The friend who bought them protested, "I saw you paint those pictures myself." Picasso answered, "I can paint fake Picassos as well as anybody."

Art and Morality: That some of the Nazis who kept the crematoria burning were moved to tears by Beethoven does not prove that music is evil, but neither, certainly, does it prove that music has great power for good.

Milton Himmelfarb
(The Jews of Modernity)

Atheism: When the atheist is confronted with one of the natural outrages against the dignity and decency of life, he is tempted to act for the moment as if God existed simply in order to have something on which to unloose his outraged feelings.

Philip Toynbee

The atheist is always alone.

Ignazio Silone

Beauty: That girl in the omnibus had one of those faces of marvelous beauty which are seen casually in the streets but never among one's friends. Where do these women come from? Who marries them? Who knows them?

Thomas Hardy

Boredom: Clemenceau was being seen off at a station by a party leader who, in his anxiety to impress the Premier, was giving him a detailed history of the political situation in France. Clemenceau, observing a man yawning on the other side of the platform, lifted his finger warningly, and said in a low voice, "I'm afraid we are overheard."

Leon Harris
(The Fine Art of Political Wit)

Celebrities: A celebrity is a person who works all his life to become well known, then wears dark glasses to avoid being recognized.

Fred Allen
(Treadmill to Oblivion)

Character: It is safer for a prince to judge men by what they do to one another than by what they do to him.

George Sevile, Marquis of Halifax
My friend, Dennis Prager, has pointed out
that if you want to know the character of
a person you are meeting socially, it is
more important to see how they act towards
the waiter, whom they are not obliged to
impress, than how they act towards you.

Clarity: The philosopher who will not take the trouble to make himself clear shows only that he thinks his thoughts of no more than academic value.

W. Somerset Maugham
(Summing Up)

Competition: Competition brings out the best in products and the worst in people.

David Sarnoff
(long-time head of R.C.A.)

Complainers: Depend upon it that if a man talks of his misfortunes, there is something in them that is not disagreeable to him.

Samuel Johnson

Conceit: The following incident will give one an idea of [Wayland's] manner in the classroom. One day, a rather conceited man said in the class when Dr. Wayland was speaking of the great wisdom of the Proverbs in the Scriptures, "I do not think there is anything very remarkable in the Proverbs. They are rather commonplace remarks of common people." "Very well," replied the Doctor. "Make one."

James Burrill Angell
(writing of Francis Wayland;
quoted in John Gardner and
Francesca Gardner Reese's
Know or Listen to Those who Know)

Consolation: A person who meets a mourner after a year, and speaks words of consolation to him then, to what can he be compared? To a physician who meets a person whose leg had been broken and healed, and says to him, "Let me break your leg again, and reset it, to convince you that my treatment was good."

Rabbi Meir
(Talmud, *Moed Katan* 21b,
translated by Francine Klagsbrun
in her book *Voices of Wisdom*)

Courage: Ten persons who speak make more noise than ten thousand who are silent.

Napoleon Bonaparte

Cowardice: While you live you dare not speak: when you die, you cannot.

Yiddish proverb

Criticism: It's a rare person who wants to hear what he doesn't want to hear.

Dick Cavett

Cynic: A cynic is a man who knows the price of everything and the value of nothing.

Oscar Wilde
(Lady Windermere's Fan)

Cynics are right nine times out of ten; what undoes them is their belief that they are right ten times out of ten.

Charles Issawi
(Issawi's Laws of Social Action)

Demagoguery: The secret of the demagogue is to make himself as stupid as his audience so that they believe they are as clever as he.

Karl Kraus

Despair: Something was dead in each of us,
And what was dead was hope.

Oscar Wilde
(The Ballad of Reading Gaol)

Dictators: So long as men worship the Caesars and Napoleons,
Caesars and Napoleons will arise to make them miserable.

Aldous Huxley
(Ends and Means)

Desires: A man can do what he wants, but not want what he wants.

Arthur Schopenhauer

Dogs: To his dog, every man is Napoleon; hence the constant popularity of dogs.

Aldous Huxley

Double Standards: If we heard it said of Orientals that they habitually drank a liquor which went to their heads, deprived them of reason and made them vomit, we should say, "How very barbarous."

La Bruyère
("Of Opinions,"
Characters, 1688)

Drama: If some great catastrophe is not announced every morning, we feel a certain void. "Nothing in the paper today," we sigh.

Paul Valéry
(cited in A. H. Auden
and Louis Kronenberger's
The Faber Book of Aphorisms)

Education: Our civilization will break down if the schools fail to teach the incoming generation that there are some things that are not done.

Gaetano Salvemini
(Italian liberal and hero
of anti-fascist movement)

Envy: We must believe in luck. For how else can we explain the success of those we don't like?

Jean Cocteau

Faith: When the heavens wish to punish a man, they take from him his faith.

Rabbi Israel Bael Shem Tov

Flattery: What really flatters a man is that you think him worth flattering.

George Bernard Shaw
(John Bull's Other Island)

Futility: Looking back at the age of eighty-eight, I see clearly that I achieved practically nothing. The world today and the history of the human anthill during the last fifty-seven years would be exactly the same if I had played Ping-Pong instead of sitting on committees and writing books and memoranda.

Leonard Woolf
(The Journey Not Arrival Matters)

Gambling: Nobody has ever bet enough on the winning horse.

cited by **Richard Sasuly**
(Bookies and Bettors)

Gratitude: If I have seen further, it is by standing on the shoulders of giants.

Isaac Newton
(letter to Robert Hooke, 1677)

Hegelian Theory: In the last century, critics of Hegelian political philosophy told me the following parable to show that Hegelian theory would be used to justify great evils. A man once saw a large sign: "Pants pressed here." He brought in his pants to be pressed, but was told: "We don't press pants here. We only make signs."

History: That men do not learn from history is the most important of all the lessons history has to teach.

Aldous Huxley
(Collected Essays)

History teaches us that men and nations behave wisely once they have exhausted all other alternatives.

Abba Eban

Humor: Humor is falling downstairs if you do it while in the act of warning your wife not to.

Kenneth Bird
(editor of *Punch*)

Innocence: The knowledge that makes us cherish innocence makes innocence unattainable.

Irving Howe
(The City in History)

Irresistible: The irresistible is often only that which is not resisted.
Justice Louis Brandeis

Judgment: It is always wise, as it is also fair, to test a man by the standards of his own day, and not by those of another.
Odell Shepard

Liquor: No man ever invented anything so bad as drunkenness – or so good as drink.

G. K. Chesterton

Loneliness: Loneliness is the first thing which God's eye named not good.

John Milton
(Tetrachordon)
Milton was referring to
Genesis 2:18: "The Lord
God said, 'It is not good
for man to be alone; I will
make a fitting helper for him'."

Machines: One machine can do the work of fifty ordinary men. No machine can do the work of one extraordinary man.

Elbert Hubbard

Martyrs: He that dies a martyr proves that he was not a knave, but by no means that he was not a fool.

Charles Caleb Cotton

The tyrant dies and his rule is over; the martyr dies and his rule begins.

Søren Kierkegaard

Money: I have never hated a man enough to give him his diamonds back.

Zsa Zsa Gabor

Money, it turned out, was exactly like sex. You thought of nothing else if you didn't have it, and thought of other things if you did.

James Baldwin
(Nobody Knows My Name)

Moral Relativism: Men who assert that all moral standards are relative, still believe that it is right to speak the truth about the relativity of moral standards.

H. Richard Niebuhr

Naïveté: I would rather be the man who bought the Brooklyn Bridge than the one who sold it.

Mark Twain

If it appears that everything is going right, you are probably unaware of all that is happening.

Earl Kulp

Neutrality: I decline utterly to be impartial as between the Fire Brigade and the Fire.

Winston Churchill

Newspapers: Everything you read in the newspapers is absolutely true, except for that rare story of which you happen to have firsthand knowledge.

Erwin Knoll
(American editor)

Originality: Millions saw the apple fall, but Newton was the one who asked why.

Bernard Baruch

Pantheism: My chief objection to pantheism is that it signifies nothing. It comes to the same thing whether you say "the world is God," or "the world is the world."

Arthur Schopenhauer
(Essays and Aphorisms)
Schopenhauer goes on to say:
"It would never occur to anyone
taking an unprejudiced view of
the world to regard it as a God.
It would clearly have to be a very
ill-advised God who knew nothing
better than to transform himself
into a world such as this one."

Patience: [G. K.] Chesterton taught me this: the only way to be sure of catching a train is to miss the one before it.

P. Daninos

Patriotism: Patriots always talk of dying for their country and never of killing for their country.

Bertrand Russell
(Autobiography)

I should like to be able to love my country and still love justice.

Albert Camus
(in a letter to a German
friend during the Hitler era)

A man who says that no patriot should attack the war until it is over is not worth answering intelligently; he is saying that no good son should warn his mother off a cliff until she has fallen over it.

G. K. Chesterton
(Orthodoxy)

Perceptions: Though time changes people, it does not alter the image we have of them.

Marcel Proust

Poverty: When a poor man eats chicken, one of them is sick.

Yiddish proverb

Progress: The reasonable man adapts himself to the world: the unreasonable one persists in trying to adapt the world to himself. Therefore, all progress depends on the unreasonable man.

George Bernard Shaw
(Maxims for Revolutionists)

Prohibition: A prohibitionist is the sort of man one wouldn't care to drink with – even if he drank.

H. L. Mencken

Proofs: We prove what we want to prove; the real difficulty lies in knowing what we want to prove.

Unknown

Quarrels: Most quarrels are inevitable at the time; incredible afterwards.

E. M. Forster

Reasons: All men have a reason, but not all men can give a reason.

John Henry Cardinal Neuman

Responsibility: Blaming others, or outside conditions for one's own misbehavior may be the child's privilege; if an adult denies responsibility for his actions, it is another step towards personality disintegration.

Bruno Bettelheim
Psychiatrist Bettelheim based
his comments on his experiences
in Nazi concentration camps.
According to Bettelheim, a
prisoner's personality disintegration became apparent the
moment he started justifying
improper behavior as due to
outside oppression.

Revolution: Most people do not go to the dentist until they have a toothache. Most societies do not reform abuses until the victims begin to make life uncomfortable to others.

Charles Issawi
(Issawi's Laws of Social Action)

Right and Wrong: Perhaps it is better to be irresponsible and right than to be responsible and wrong.

Winston Churchill

Ruthlessness: What millions died that Caesar might be great.

Thomas Campbell
(The Pleasures of Hope)

Sabbath: The Sabbath is what you make of it – a holy day, a holiday, a rest day, a sports day – or, if you're not smart, another work day.

Rabbi Herbert Goldstein

Self-Alienation: What have I in common with other Jews? I have hardly anything in common with myself and should stand very quietly in a corner, content that I can breathe.

Franz Kafka
(Diaries)

Self-Assessment: My time has not yet come; some men are born posthumously.

Friedrich Nietzsche
(Ecce Homo)

Self-Confidence: I can't make people like me but if I wasn't me I would like me.

Anonymous third-grader
(in Brooklyn Avenue School,
Valley Stream, New York;
quoted in James Simpson's
Contemporary Quotations)

Self-Control: I have heard people argue that they have no control over their emotions. But if they would take an objective observation of themselves, they would realize to what extent they do have control when they really wish. For example, when they have lost their temper at a member of their family, they might scream and shout, and claim they cannot help it. But if someone they want to impress knocks on the door in the middle of their tantrum, they will be able to answer the door and immediately talk calmly and pleasantly.

Rabbi Zelig Pliskin
(Gateway to Happiness)

Self-Destructiveness: What kills a skunk is the publicity it gives itself.

Abraham Lincoln
(on slavery)

When iron was created the trees began to tremble. The iron said to them: "Why do you tremble. Let none of your wood [be used in making my handle], and not one of you will be injured."

Rabbinic text
(Genesis Rabbah, 5:10)

Self-Hatred: I wouldn't want to belong to any club that would accept me as a member.

Groucho Marx
(in telegram resigning
club membership)

Self-Righteousness: You are not as good as you think you are. And the world is not as bad as you think it is.

Rabbi Wolf of Strikov

Serenity: A Jewish legend tells that **King Solomon** once approached a jeweler with an unusual request. He asked that the man design a ring on which would be inscribed words that would be true and appropriate at all times and in all situations. The jeweler brought the king a ring on which was inscribed, "This too shall pass." In times of pain, the king looked at the ring and was reassured. In times of joy and exultation the king looked at the ring and felt sobered.

Slavery: If slavery is not wrong, nothing is wrong.

Abraham Lincoln
(April 4, 1864)

Sports: When you win you're an old pro. When you lose you're an old man.

Charlie Conerly
(quarterback for the New York Giants)
During the 1960 presidential campaign,
the forty-three-year-old John F.
Kennedy met the great St. Louis
Cardinal outfielder, Stan Musial,
then in his late thirties. Kennedy
remarked, "They say you're too
old to run, and I'm too young."

I always turn to the sports page first. The sports page records people's accomplishments; the front page nothing but men's failures.

Chief Justice Earl Warren

Statistics: A dog run over by a car upsets our emotional balance.... Three million Jews killed in Poland causes but a moderate uneasiness. Statistics don't bleed: it is the detail which counts.

Arthur Koestler
("On Observing Atrocities,"
in *The Yogi and the Commisar
and Other Essays*)

Television: Television has proved that people will look at anything rather than each other.
Ann Landers

All television is educational television. The question is: what is it teaching?

Nicholas Johnson
(former member of the Federal
Communications Commission)

Temptation: I can resist everything except temptation.
Oscar Wilde
(Lady Windermere's Fan)

Time: I wish I could stand on a busy corner, hat in hand, and beg people to throw me all their wasted hours.
Bernard Berenson

A man who has taken your time recognizes no debt, yet it is the only debt he can never repay.

Anonymous

Tips: I wonder if it ain't just cowardice, instead of generosity, that makes us give most of our tips.

Will Rogers

Tragedy: In a true tragedy, both parties must be right.

Georg Wilhelm Hegel

Universe: Leave only three wasps alive in the whole of Europe, and . . . Europe will still be more crowded with wasps than space is with stars.

James Jeans

Value: If you sell diamonds, you cannot expect to have many customers. But a diamond is a diamond even if there are no customers.

Swami Prabhupada

Victory: Victory has a hundred fathers, and defeat is an orphan.

John F. Kennedy
(following the failure of the Bay
of Pigs invasion of Cuba in 1961,
after proponents of the invasion
denied all responsibility)